Children's
WEATHER
Encyclopedia

Discover the science behind our planet's weather

PaRragon

Bath·New York·Singapore·Hong Kong·Cologne·Delhi·Melbourne

Author: Louise Spilsbury

Consultant: John Williams

This edition produced by Tall Tree Ltd, London

First published by Parragon in 2007

Parragon
Queen Street House
4 Queen Street
Bath BA1 1HE, UK

Copyright © Parragon Books Ltd 2007

ISBN 978-1-4054-9554-7

Printed in China

Children's
WEATHER
Encyclopedia

Discover the science behind our planet's weather

Louise Spilsbury

Bath · New York · Singapore · Hong Kong · Cologne · Delhi · Melbourne

CONTENTS

INTRODUCTION

Our planet is surrounded by a layer of gases that make up the atmosphere. This layer is always moving, as heat from the sun warms certain parts of the surface more than others. This movement brings with it the many weather conditions. The type of weather you experience can vary greatly, from hot, dry summers to freezing blizzards, and from torrential storms to calm days with just a slight breeze. The weather can make a region rich—the right conditions can make crops ripen and flourish. Extreme weather systems, however, can be violent, causing millions of dollars' worth of damage.

WHAT IS WEATHER?

The weather affects almost everything you do, from the food you eat to the clothes you wear and the sports you play. Just think about the number of times a week you talk about the weather. It is all around you, all the time! In this chapter, you will discover what causes the weather and find out all the important weather facts—including how snowflakes form, why rain falls, what hail is, and what makes the winds blow.

How weather affects us

The weather is an important part of our lives. It affects us in many ways—from what we wear to the way we feel. Wet weather may stop us from playing outside, while sunshine may mean a day at the beach.

Weather conditions

The word "weather" describes the conditions in the air around us at a particular time and place. For example, the air may be warm or cold, wet or dry, still or windy. One of the reasons why weather is so important to us is that it comes in so many different forms, such as rain, snow, sleet, hail, fog, mist, sunshine, wind, and cloud—all of which affect us in different ways.

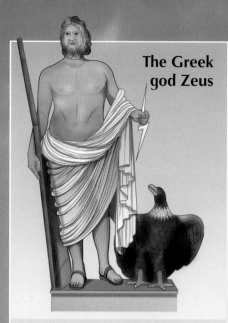

The Greek god Zeus

Weather gods

In the past, people worshipped weather gods. In ancient Greece, the people believed that Zeus controlled the weather. He was often shown holding a bolt of lightning.

Protecting ourselves

Many of the clothes we wear are designed to protect us from some of the effects of the weather. For example, hats shield us from the heat of the summer sunshine and keep our heads warm in winter. Umbrellas help us stay dry in the rain, and coats, gloves, and scarves stop our body heat escaping into the chilly air on a cold day.

Sudden changes

In some places, the weather changes very little for weeks or months at a time. For example, on the equator, the imaginary line around the middle of Earth, the weather is hot and rainy all year. In many other places, the weather can change from one minute to the next and from day to day. For example, in some parts of the United States, one day may be dry and sunny, while the next is wet and cold.

Top Facts

- Temperature is measured in degrees Farenheit (°F). Water freezes at 32 degrees Farenheit and boils at 212 degrees Farenheit. Temperatures below 0 degrees Farenheit have a minus sign before them.

- Other countries use a different temperature scale, which is called Celsius (°C). Water freezes at 0 degrees Celsius and boils at 100 degrees Celsius.

Weather and our mood

The weather can even affect our mood. A sunny day can make us feel happy, while a cloudy day can make us feel sad. This is probably because our brains are stimulated by sunlight. People who feel miserable during the winter sometimes have an illness called Seasonal Affective Disorder (SAD). Many use sun lamps (pictured) to help with this problem.

It's Amazing!

In Botswana in Africa, rain is so important to the wealth of the country that the national currency is called the "pula," which means "rain" or "blessing!"

The Sun

The Sun is a giant ball of burning gas that lies millions of miles from Earth. It produces a massive amount of energy that heats Earth and powers the winds, the seasons, and all of our weather. The Sun's energy also makes our planet the right temperature for life to exist.

Solar energy

Energy from the Sun travels through space to Earth in straight lines called rays. These rays travel at the speed of light, which is about 186,000 miles per second. Even so, the rays take about eight minutes to reach Earth. We can see some of the Sun's energy as light, but a lot of the energy given off by the Sun is invisible. Infrared rays from the Sun heat up Earth but can't be seen by the naked eye. Ultraviolet, or UV, rays are invisible but will tan and even burn skin that is exposed to sunlight.

Sunset over the Masai Mara, Kenya

Heat in the core

The temperature at the core, or center, of the Sun is about 28.8 million°F. This heat energy flows slowly to the surface of the Sun and then travels across space to Earth.

The Sun

Top Facts

- Never look directly at the Sun! It is so bright that the light could badly damage your eyes, and even make you blind.

- The Sun is a star. All stars produce vast amounts of light and heat energy.

- Without the Sun, there would be no life on Earth.

Giant ball of gas

The Sun is so enormous that a million Earths could fit inside it! This huge ball of burning gas is 93 million miles from Earth, which is close enough to keep our planet warm but not so hot that water boils away into a gas. Instead, water can exist as a liquid and as a solid (in the form of ice). Liquid water is essential to life.

Sun
870,000 miles in diameter

Earth
7,926 miles in diameter

Jupiter
89,928 miles in diameter

The right temperature

Less than a millionth of the Sun's energy reaches Earth. Most of the Sun's heat is reflected by the blanket of gases around Earth called the atmosphere. Some of the heat reaches Earth but bounces off the surface and back into space. This helps to keep Earth cool enough for life to exist.

Sunbathing

As well as being important for our weather, sunlight is good for us in small quantities. Our bodies need sunlight to make vitamin D, which is important for healthy growth. However, we should not spend too long sunbathing, because it can also damage our skin.

It's Amazing!

The Sun is 5 billion years old, and heat from its core can take a million years to reach the surface. At the surface, the temperature is more than 500 times hotter than the temperature of boiling water.

In the sky

The atmosphere is a mixture of gases that surrounds Earth, similar to the way the peel of an orange surrounds the fruit. The atmosphere is held around Earth by the force of gravity.

Layers of the atmosphere

The atmosphere is made up of five main layers. The troposphere is the lowest layer, which contains 90 percent of all the air. Above it is the stratosphere, then the mesosphere and the thermosphere. Finally, there is the exosphere, which gradually fades into space.

Gases in the atmosphere

The air in the troposphere is made up of nitrogen and oxygen, as well as a tiny amount of other gases, such as argon and carbon dioxide. We, and many other living things, need to breathe air to live. Our bodies use oxygen to make energy.

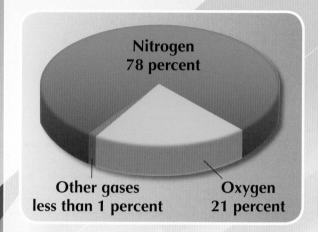

Nitrogen
78 percent

Other gases
less than 1 percent

Oxygen
21 percent

Stratosphere
10–30 miles above
the surface

Meteors

Airplane

Troposphere
0–10 miles
above the surface

Weather balloon

Mesosphere
30–50 miles above
the surface

Protective layer

The atmosphere protects Earth from meteors, or space rocks, most of which burn up before they crash into Earth. They can be seen as streaks of light in the night sky. The atmosphere also protects Earth from the Sun's harmful rays.

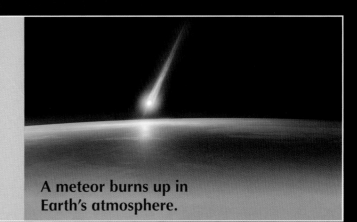

A meteor burns up in Earth's atmosphere.

It's Amazing!

The total weight of Earth's atmosphere is about 4.5 billion tons! The weight of the air pushing down on Earth's surface is called air pressure.

Out of breath

Most of the air is near to Earth's surface. The higher you go in the atmosphere, the more the gas reduces, or thins. Animals that live on high land, such as llamas, have to be able to breathe this "thinner" air.

Llamas graze in the Andes Mountains in Peru.

Aurorae

Exosphere
more than 280 miles
above the surface

The weather layer

All of Earth's weather occurs in the troposphere. As well as having most of the air in the atmosphere, the troposphere also contains water in the form of a gas called water vapor. This water vapor cools and collects together into water droplets to form clouds. Jet airplanes fly just above the troposphere to avoid the clouds.

Thermosphere
50–280 miles above
the surface

Clouds

When seen from space, Earth looks like a blue ball covered by swirls of white clouds. These clouds are created when heat from the Sun warms up the air, making it rise.

What clouds are

Clouds form when water vapor in the air condenses, or turns into liquid, and becomes tiny droplets of water. The droplets are so small and light that they can float in the air. When billions of these droplets come together, they form a cloud.

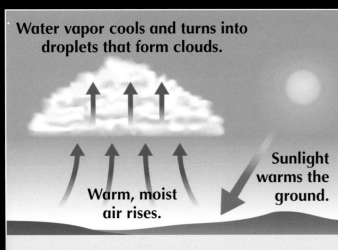

Water vapor cools and turns into droplets that form clouds.

Warm, moist air rises.

Sunlight warms the ground.

Cloud formation

The Sun heats Earth's surface, which warms the air just above the surface. The warm air rises, cooling as it does so. As it cools, the water vapor in the air turns into droplets, forming clouds.

It's Amazing!

Weather satellites that take photographs of the clouds from space are in orbit about 22,300 miles above the planet.

Mountain clouds

When air moves toward a mountain, it is forced upward by the mountain side. As the air rises, it cools and forms clouds. That is why the tops of mountains are often covered by clouds.

Clouds form over Mount Taranaki in New Zealand.

Cloud colors

All clouds, whether white or gray, partly shade the ground from sunlight. Clouds are white because the droplets of water in them reflect the sunlight shining from above. Clouds turn gray when there are so many water droplets in them that they stop sunlight getting through and reaching the surface.

Vapor trails left by a high-flying jet

Vapor trails

The white trails behind a plane are artificial clouds. The exhaust fumes from the hot engines are full of water vapor. The vapor cools when it hits the cold air outside, creating the trails made of ice crystals.

Top Facts

- The point at which water vapor forms water droplets is called the dew point.

- Clouds help to insulate Earth by stopping some of its heat from escaping into space.

- Clouds also keep Earth cool by blocking some of the Sun's energy.

Name that cloud

There are three main types of cloud: cirrus, cumulus, and stratus. These main types can combine to form other types of cloud. There are about ten different varieties in all.

Highest clouds

The highest clouds are usually thin, wispy cirrus clouds. They form in the troposphere at heights of more than 9 miles. It is very cold there, and the water in the clouds freezes to form ice crystals.

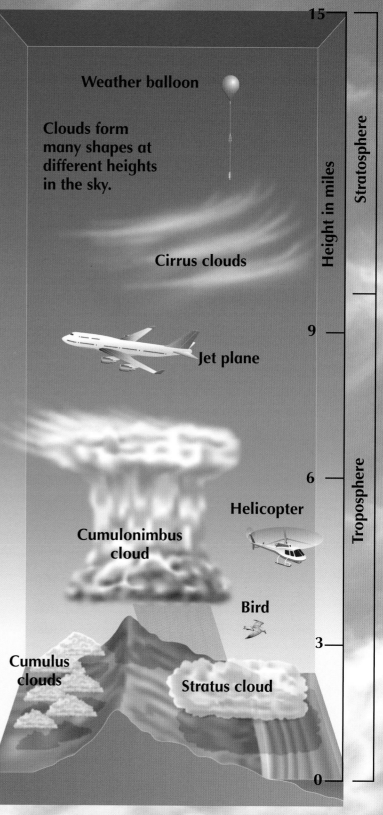

Clouds form many shapes at different heights in the sky.

Weather balloon

Cirrus clouds

Jet plane

Cumulonimbus cloud

Helicopter

Bird

Cumulus clouds

Stratus cloud

Height in miles

Stratosphere

Troposphere

15

9

6

3

0

Cumulus clouds

Good weather clouds

Many people think that clouds are a sign of rain, but some clouds can be a sign of good weather. Cumulus clouds in the sky mean that the weather will be dry.

Nimbostratus clouds

Rain clouds

Rain falls from clouds that are low in the sky and contain liquid water droplets instead of frozen ice crystals. Some rain clouds have the word "nimbus" added to their name. They include the dark gray nimbostratus clouds.

Cloud namer

In 1802, the British scientist Luke Howard (1772–1864) developed a way of classifying, or grouping, clouds. We still use the Latin words he chose to describe their characteristics.

- "Cirrus" means "a tuft or filament."
- "Cumulus" means "a heap or pile."
- "Stratus" means "a layer."
- "Nimbus" means "rain bearing."

Cotton-ball clouds

Cumulus clouds form lower down in the atmosphere than cirrus clouds. They are sometimes called cotton-ball clouds because they form lumpy white clusters. Cumulus clouds often form on a summer's day and will disappear quickly in the warm sunshine, leaving a clear blue sky. At the same level or below the cumulus clouds are the stratus clouds. These look like gray blankets of cloud, lying low in the sky. They often bring damp, drizzly weather.

It's Amazing!

Cumulonimbus storm clouds can be 6 miles wide and 6 miles high. These monster clouds are full of energy, and the winds that develop inside them can reach speeds of 125 miles per hour.

Storm clouds

Cumulonimbus clouds form when more and more rising air joins a cumulus cloud. These clouds can bring hail, heavy rain, thunder, and lightning—causing sudden floods.

Cumulonimbus clouds

Rain

The water that falls from the sky as rain is vital for life on our planet. Rain fills rivers, lakes, and reservoirs, providing water for people and animals to drink. It waters the land so that plants can grow. Without rain, there would be no life on Earth.

The water cycle

Rain is part of the water cycle. This is the process by which water circulates between the ground and the sky. When water on the land and at the surface of lakes, rivers, and seas is warmed by sunshine, some of it evaporates. This means it turns from liquid water into a gas called water vapor. The water vapor then cools and turns back into water droplets to form clouds. The water falls as rain, snow, or hail.

Top Facts

- The average diameter of a raindrop is $1/25$ to $1/12$ inch.
- Drizzle is rain that falls in tiny drops measuring less than $1/50$ inch.
- Most raindrops fall at a speed of between 10 and 25 feet per second.

Sun

Sunshine warms the surface water in rivers, lakes, oceans, and on land, causing it to evaporate into water vapor.

Evaporation

Rivers flow into lakes or the ocean.

Water evaporates from moist soil and plants.

Evaporation

It's Amazing!

In 2004, scientists saw monster raindrops about $1/3$ inch wide in clouds over Brazil and the Marshall Islands—a group of small islands in the central Pacific Ocean.

Some water seeps through the ground into lakes or the sea.

Water in the air

There is a huge amount of water in the troposphere. Every single day, more than 900 billion tons of water evaporates into the air from the oceans alone. When ocean water evaporates, it leaves the salt behind, so rain water is fresh water not salty.

Clouds form as the air rises and cools.

Rain falls from clouds.

Some rain seeps into the ground.

Rain fills rivers.

How rain forms

Inside a cloud, swirling winds blow water droplets around. When the water droplets bump into each other, they join together. Eventually, the droplets become heavy enough and start to fall. As they fall, the droplets gather more moisture to form even larger raindrops. Small raindrops are almost spherical, or round, in shape. Larger drops are flattened at the bottom, similar to hamburger rolls.

Dirty rain

As water vapor in the atmosphere cools, it is attracted to dust particles, some of which are released by factories and homes. The water vapor joins to the dust particles to form droplets of dirty water.

Particles released from a power station in Great Britain.

Snow and hail

Most of us love to see snowflakes falling from the sky, covering the ground in white powder. Snow and hail are both forms of precipitation that fall during cold weather. Raindrops are liquid water, but snow and hail are made of water that has frozen solid to form ice.

How hail forms

Hail is a shower of frozen raindrops. The hail forms inside large cumulonimbus clouds. The fast winds inside these clouds blow the raindrops so high that they freeze into small balls of ice called hailstones. As these balls swirl around inside the cloud, they pick up more water, which freezes into layers of ice around them, making them grow bigger. Eventually, the hailstones become so heavy that they fall from the cloud to the ground.

Hail damage

Hail storms are often very destructive. Hailstones can smash windows and damage crops, including this farmer's sunflowers. In the United States, about 450 million dollars' worth of damage is caused by hailstones every year.

Snow settles on the ground and trees when the temperature is cold enough to stop it from melting.

Giant hailstones

The largest hailstone ever recorded measured 18 $\frac{1}{3}$ inches in diameter. The heaviest weighed about 2 pounds. These giants formed when strong winds delayed the hailstones from falling to the ground, so they kept getting bigger.

A hailstone that is almost the size of a golf ball

A farmer in North Dakota studies his hail-damaged crop.

Why snow falls

Snow forms when the temperature is so cold that water vapor in a cloud freezes. It forms tiny ice crystals that stick together to form snowflakes. When the snowflakes are big and heavy enough, they fall to the ground as snow. The snowflakes fall at different speeds depending on their size. A typical snowflake travels to the ground at about 3 feet per second.

It's Amazing!

The largest snowflake ever recorded fell on Fort Keogh, Montana on January 28, 1887. It was 15 inches across!

Top Facts

- Glaciers are sheets of ice that form when snow builds up on the ground and slowly turns to ice.

- If the air near the ground is too warm, snow melts as it falls and turns to rain.

- If you cut open a hailstone, you will see the layers of ice as rings. These rings tell you how many times the hailstone has moved up and down inside a cloud.

Snowflakes

An individual snowflake may be made up of up to 200 ice crystals. No two snowflakes are identical. The shape of a snowflake depends on the temperature and the way it falls through the sky.

Frost and dew

Frost and dew form in the mornings after clear, still nights. On these nights, the land cools quickly and becomes colder than the air above it. This is called temperature inversion.

Blanket of frost

Frost forms when water vapor close to the ground comes into contact with very cold surfaces. When this happens, the water vapor in the air turns straight into ice crystals. These ice crystals settle in a blanket of white frost on leaves and fields.

It's Amazing!

Hot water freezes more quickly than cold water! That is why people who want to remove ice from their car windshield should pour cold water instead of hot water over the window.

Frost damage to a crop of tangerines in Florida

Frost damage

Frost freezes the water in plants and damages them. The damaged plants turn black and often die. Gardeners sometimes use heaters to protect their plants from frost.

Frost fairs

Frost fairs were carnivals held on the icy surface of the River Thames in London, England. The first frost fair was held in 1607. The climate in Europe between about 1500 and 1850 was known as the Little Ice Age because the winters were so cold that rivers froze over each year. The last frost fair was held on the Thames in 1814.

Frostbite

When a person's flesh freezes, they have frostbite. Blood stops flowing to the frozen flesh. Sometimes, frostbitten toes and fingers have to be cut off because the flesh is dead. Mountain climbers take great care to prevent frostbite.

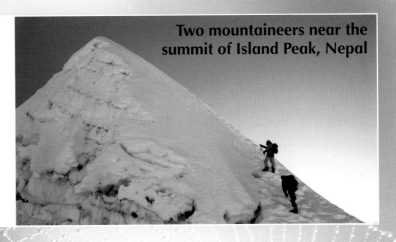

Two mountaineers near the summit of Island Peak, Nepal

Morning dew

During the night, the air near the ground is full of water vapor. The ground cools down at night when the Sun is not shining, and this may make the water in the air condense and collect into water droplets. Because the droplets of water are close to the ground, they often gather on grass, leaves, and spiders' webs. This is what we call dew.

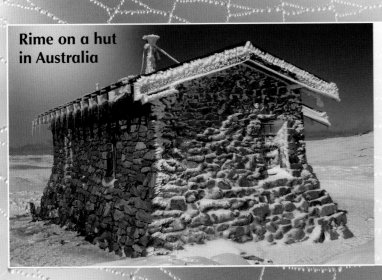

Rime on a hut in Australia

Rime

Rime is a kind of thick, white frost that appears on cold, foggy days. The very cold water droplets in the fog (see pages 26–27) freeze when they come into contact with solid objects. Rime forms a crusty coating of ice crystals on the surface of branches, buildings, and even cyclists who ride into cold winds.

Fog and mist

Mist and fog are clouds of tiny water droplets that hang close to the ground. Mist and fog are not classed as precipitation because the water droplets do not fall. Instead, they are light enough to remain floating in the air.

Making mist and fog

Mist and fog are the same as clouds, but they form near ground level. This happens when water vapor from lakes, oceans, and rivers or moist soil and plants meets colder air. It then cools to the point where it changes into water droplets small enough to be carried on gentle air currents.

Mountain gorillas live on the mountains of central Africa, where mists occur frequently.

Sea fog

Sea fog forms when warm air that contains a lot of water vapor blows over colder sea water. The water vapor in the air cools and condenses to form a fog of tiny water droplets.

Sea fog forms off the coast of Oregon.

Make your own fog

- Ask an adult to fill a jar with warm water.
- Let the jar stand for about a minute, then pour out most of the water, leaving a little in the bottom.
- Hold a sieve with three ice cubes in it close to the top of the jar.
- When the cold air from the ice cubes meets the warm, moist air in the jar, it forms a small cloud of fog.

Heavy traffic caught in fog

Fog problems

Fog reduces the distance drivers can see in front of them, especially at night. That is why traffic police warn drivers to slow down in fog or avoid traveling altogether.

Seeing in fog and mist

Fog is thicker than mist because it contains more water droplets than mist. Mist becomes fog when the visibility, or how far you can see, is less than 1,100 yards. Fog and mist usually form at night or early in the morning and disappear during the day. In colder climates, however, where fog is more common, it may last all day.

Haze and smog

Haze is like mist but it is made up of tiny particles of dust, smoke, or salt instead of water droplets. Although the particles in haze are too small to see individually, together they cause a slight reduction in visibility. A smog (see page 202) is a thick haze, where the visibility is extremely poor.

A haze of smog hangs over the city of Los Angeles.

It's Amazing!

In December 2006, thick fog caused the cancellation of almost all flights out of Heathrow airport in Great Britain. Nearly 800,000 people who had planned to travel home to their families or abroad for a vacation were affected by delays and cancellations.

Wind

Wind is the movement of air over the surface of Earth. Different parts of the surface get different amounts of heat from sunlight, and it is these differences in temperature that cause wind.

How winds form

When sunlight warms the ground, the air above the ground heats up and rises. Because the air is rising, it is not pushing down on the ground so the air pressure is low. The rising air then cools, sinks, and pushes down on the ground, creating high pressure. As the cool air sinks, it pushes the air below from an area of high pressure to an area of low pressure. This moving air is wind.

Sea breezes

Land heats up faster than water. This means that, during the day, the air above the land is warm and rises. Cooler air from over the sea rushes in, creating a cooling sea breeze.

Yachts race off the island of St. Thomas in the Caribbean.

Create air pressure

- Blow up a balloon and keep the end closed. Release the balloon and watch it fly around!

- The air inside the inflated balloon is squeezed under high pressure. When you release the balloon, the air rushes out and pushes the balloon forward.

Beaufort Scale

Wind speeds are sometimes measured using a system called the Beaufort Scale. The scale runs from 0 (calm) to 12 (hurricane).

Category		Description
	0	Calm
	1	Light air
	2	Light breeze
	3	Gentle breeze
	4	Moderate breeze
	5	Fresh breeze
	6	Strong breeze
	7	Near gale
	8	Gale
	9	Strong gale
	10	Storm
	11	Violent storm
	12	Hurricane

Wind and waves

When wind blows across an ocean, it pulls on the water at the surface. The surface water rises, but is pulled back down by gravity, forming waves. A strong wind will form large waves.

A yacht's sails catch the wind, pushing the boat across the water.

A jumbo jet takes off.

Turbulence

Turbulence happens when winds move up and down suddenly. It can be caused by storm clouds or strong winds over mountains. Planes can be affected by turbulence.

Worldwide winds

The winds that blow around the world follow regular patterns. These patterns are affected by Earth's rotation, the seasons, and the position of the land, as well as by physical features, such as mountains.

Asia

Northeast trade

Monsoon

Southeast trade

Australasia

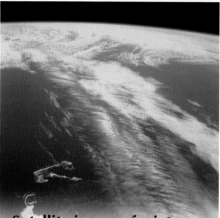

Satellite image of a jet stream over Canada

It's Amazing!

The expression "in the doldrums," meaning "depressed," comes from winds. There is a region near the equator where the winds are very light. Ships can't sail without wind, so sailors named the region the doldrums.

Jet streams

Jet streams are channels of fast-flowing air high in the troposphere. These tunnels of wind are thousands of miles long and hundreds of miles wide. Winds in the jet streams travel at speeds of up to 185 miles per hour.

The Coriolis effect

As Earth spins, the rotation bends the winds. This is called the Coriolis effect. If Earth did not spin, winds from the poles would blow straight toward the equator, but the Coriolis effect bends these winds to the right in the Northern Hemisphere and to the left in the Southern Hemisphere.

The Rocky Mountains in North America

Chinook

A chinook is a warm wind that blows down the Rocky Mountains in North America. Its name means "snow eater" because the wind melts the snow.

Wind patterns in January

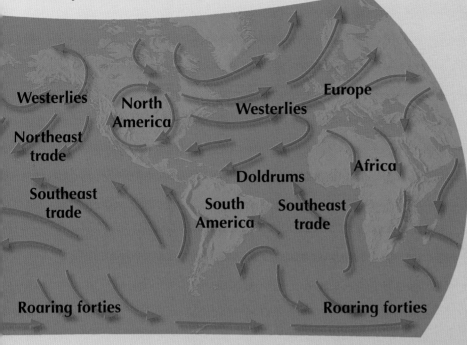

Westerlies

North America

Europe

Westerlies

Northeast trade

Africa

Doldrums

Southeast trade

South America

Southeast trade

Roaring forties

Roaring forties

Trade winds

The winds that blow from the east near the equator are known as the Trade Winds. They were named hundreds of years ago when most of the world's trade was carried by sailing ships. These winds helped ships sail the oceans, carrying goods for buying and selling.

Naming winds

Winds are named after the direction from which they blow. So a wind called a "Westerly" will blow from the west and a wind called a "Southeast Trade" will blow from the southeast. The regular patterns that these winds blow over Earth changes slightly throughout the year as the seasons change.

Wind patterns in July

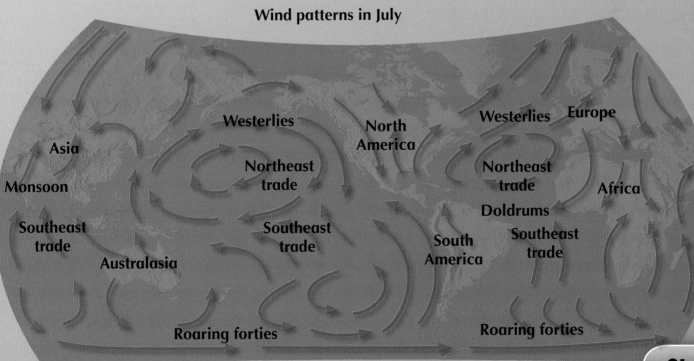

Westerlies

North America

Westerlies

Europe

Asia

Northeast trade

Northeast trade

Africa

Monsoon

Doldrums

Southeast trade

Southeast trade

South America

Southeast trade

Australasia

Roaring forties

Roaring forties

Special effects

From colorful rainbows to red sunsets, the weather fills the sky with different colors. These special effects are created by light reacting with the weather, such as rain or heat, or with particles in the troposphere.

Why is the sky blue?

Light from sunshine may appear to be white, but it is actually a combination of the seven colors of the spectrum: red, orange, yellow, green, blue, indigo, and violet. When sunlight passes through the troposphere, light rays reflect, or bounce, off gas and dust in the air and are scattered. The sky looks blue on a sunny day because blue is scattered more in the air than the other colors in light are.

Red sky

At sunset and sunrise, sunlight travels farther through the atmosphere than when the sun is overhead. Only red light is not scattered by the air and dust, making the sky appear red.

A rainbow in the sky over Colorado

It's Amazing!

Light is formed of many more than seven colors, but these main ones are the best known. However, only one person in every thousand can see indigo, which is a dark blue color between blue and violet.

Make your own rainbow!

- Standing with your back to the sun on a bright day, spray water from a plant sprayer or a water hose by partly covering the end with your finger.

- You should see a rainbow form in the water spray.

Mirages

Mirages are tricks of the light that often occur in hot places. When light rays, which usually travel in straight lines, move into hot air near the land from cool air above, they are refracted, or bent. The bent light makes an image of an object appear below it. For example, an image of a tree on the sand makes it look as if there is an upside-down tree in the desert.

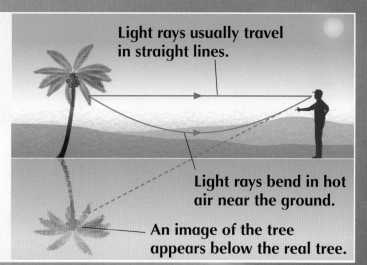

Light rays usually travel in straight lines.

Light rays bend in hot air near the ground.

An image of the tree appears below the real tree.

How rainbows form

A prism is a wedge-shaped piece of glass that splits sunlight into the seven colors of the spectrum. Rainbows form when light from the sun comes into contact with droplets of water in the air. The water droplets act like mini prisms and split light into many colors. We see rainbows when the rain is in front of us and the sun is behind us and low in the sky.

Northern lights in the sky over Wisconsin

Northern lights

The *aurora borealis*, or northern lights, are displays of colored lights in the sky above northern countries. The sun gives off billions of tiny, very energetic particles. When these react with particles high in the atmosphere, they create glowing multicolored swirls.

CLIMATE

The weather in the place where you live probably changes throughout the year. Although the weather changes, it usually follows a particular pattern. For example, a region may have cold winters and warm summers. This regular pattern of weather is known as the climate. The climate of a place varies for many reasons, including where it is, how near or far from the ocean it is, how much sunlight it gets, and how high it is above sea level.

What is climate?

People have kept records for hundreds of years of the temperature and rainfall in different places. The word "climate" describes the average pattern of weather in a particular place on our planet. The weather is what it is like outside on a particular day.

Humidity

The humidity tells us how much water vapor there is in the air. Warm air contains more water than cold air. We feel hotter and sweatier in humid air because water vapor stops our sweat from evaporating, which would normally cool us down.

Temperature

The temperature is a major part of the climate. In some climates, the temperature goes up and down throughout the day and year, but in others it remains more constant. People use thermometers to measure temperature. Thermometers show the temperature as numbers of units called degrees Fahrenheit (°F) or degrees Celsius (°C).

Temperature range

Different climates have different temperature ranges. On tropical grasslands (see pages 52–53) the range is small as the temperature is constant all year. On temperate grasslands (see pages 50–51), where it is warm in summer and cold in winter, the range is large.

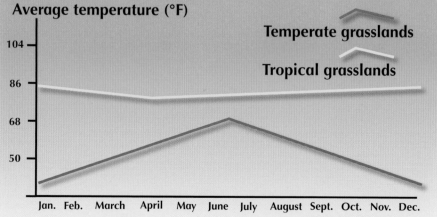

Average temperature (°F)

Temperate grasslands

Tropical grasslands

104

86

68

50

Jan. Feb. March April May June July August Sept. Oct. Nov. Dec.

Precipitation

Another major part of the climate is precipitation—the water that falls to the ground in the form of rain, snow, or hail. Precipitation is measured in inches or millimetres falling over a particular amount of time, such as a day or a month.

Air-conditioning

In 1902, US engineer Willis Carrier designed an air-conditioning device to make life in humid climates more pleasant. His invention passed humid air over coolers to lower the temperature. The process also caused the water vapor in the air to condense, making the air drier. Air conditioning is used in buildings and vehicles all over the world.

It's Amazing!

The biggest daily temperature range ever recorded was in Loma, Montana in 1972. In just 24 hours, the temperature rose by 103 degrees Farenheit.

Wind chill

We feel colder when it is windy, even if the air temperature has not changed. This is called wind chill. It happens because wind makes our bodies lose heat more quickly. The colder the temperature, the more the wind chill affects us.

A mountain resort in Spain, where the climate will be cold in winter, but it may be hot in the summer

Hot or cold?

The amount of heat the Sun produces is always about the same. How hot or cold a place is depends on its position on Earth as the planet spins and travels around the Sun. Winds and ocean currents affect the climate by moving heat around the planet.

The angle of sunlight

The main reason for temperature differences on the ground is that the planet is spherical, or ball-shaped. Sunlight travels to our planet in straight lines. It strikes the equator at a right angle, and the concentrated heat produces a warm climate there. At the poles, the sunlight hits the ground at a low angle. This means the heat is spread over a wider area, resulting in a cold climate.

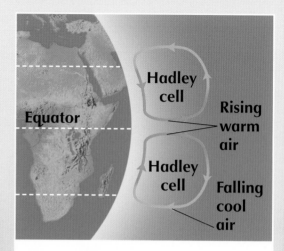

Air circulation

Air heated at the equator rises and spreads out high in the troposphere. It then cools and sinks to the surface, where it is pushed back to the equator. These circular air currents are called Hadley cells.

Sand dunes in the Sahara, Africa

Heat haze above a road in the Atacama Desert, Chile

Heat haze

Areas of concrete or tarmac, such as roads, absorb more heat during the day than their surroundings. These areas heat up and warm the air above them, creating a shimmering heat haze.

Ocean currents

Winds blowing over the surface of the oceans create surface ocean currents, which are like giant rivers moving through the sea. These currents may be cold or warm, depending on where they form. Cold currents usually bring cooler weather to the land they pass and warm currents usually bring warmer weather.

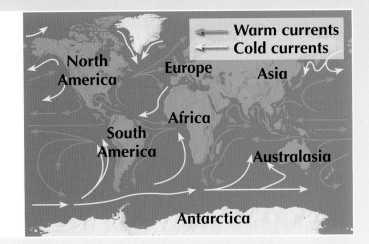

Warm currents
Cold currents

North America
Europe
Asia
Africa
South America
Australasia
Antarctica

A large iceberg in the Arctic Ocean near Greenland

It's Amazing!
The circulation of heat around the planet makes the temperatures less extreme. Without it, the equator would be 25 degrees Farenheit warmer and the poles would be 45 degrees Farenheit colder.

Spinning Earth

Earth rotates once on its axis every 24 hours. Places facing the Sun are warmer than those facing away, so nights are colder than days. Earth's axis is not vertical but at an angle. This means that different points on the surface are closer to the Sun at different times of year as the planet makes its yearly orbit around the Sun. This tilt creates the seasons (see pages 62–63).

Surface features

The planet's surface varies greatly, from flat plains and towering peaks to immense oceans with no land in sight. These surface features affect the climate. For example, mountain areas are usually colder than coastal regions.

Altitude and aspect

The climate in a place at high altitude, which is many miles above sea level, is usually colder than at sea level. This is why there is often snow on mountaintops even in hot climates. Mountain slopes facing toward the sunlight are warmer than those facing away. This is called aspect.

Atacama bodies

The Atacama Desert in Chile is the driest place on the planet. There, the buried remains of dead people do not rot in the dry soil. Scientists have discovered the remains of preserved bodies in the Atacama Desert that are more than 7,000 years old.

Rain shadow desert

Direction of wind

Green fertile land

Sea

Moist air rises up the slope and cools, producing clouds and rain.

Air that reaches the far side of the mountain is dry because all its moisture has already fallen as rain.

Rain shadows

Rain shadows are dry regions that form on one side of a mountain range. Water vapor in air blowing from the sea cools as it rises up the mountain slope and falls as rain. The air that reaches the far side of the mountain is therefore dry, creating a desert on that side. The Atacama Desert in South America is a rain shadow desert.

Distance from the ocean

Land heats up and cools down faster than the ocean because rocks and soil absorb less heat than water. This means that places on the coast have warmer winters and cooler summers than places inland. This difference is called continentality.

Kilimanjaro in Tanzania, Africa

Snow on the summit of Kilimanjaro

Macaque monkeys in a hot spring in Nagano, Japan

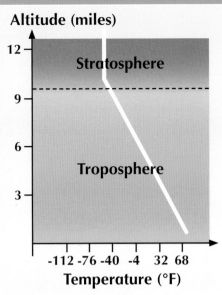

Altitude (miles)

Stratosphere

Troposphere

-112 -76 -40 -4 32 68

Temperature (°F)

Going up

As you climb higher in the troposphere, the temperature drops up to 17.5°F for every 3,300 feet you ascend. This is because the amount of air decreases, or gets thin, as the altitude increases, and thinner air cannot hold as much heat. That is why the tops of the highest mountains are very cold.

Microclimates

A very small area with a different climate from its surroundings is said to have a microclimate. This is often because of a particular surface feature. For example, hot springs in a cold mountain create a warm microclimate.

It's Amazing!

Scientists studying ancient rocks in the Atacama Desert have discovered that some parts of the desert have never had a drop of rain!

Climate zones

The world can be divided into several climate zones, each with a particular pattern of weather. The zones help us understand the world's climate, but the weather within the zones can vary.

Key

- Polar climates
- Continental climates
- Temperate climates
- Dry climates
- Tropical climates

The main zones

Scientists split the world into five major climate zones. Polar climates have freezing temperatures all year round. Continental climates have cold winters and hot summers. Temperate areas have cool winters and warm summers. Dry climates have very little rain. Tropical areas have hot, wet climates.

It's Amazing!
The Greek scholar Aristotle, who lived more than 2,000 years ago, was the first to classify the world's climate. He thought the climate at the equator was too hot to live in!

The Arctic

North America

South America

Tropical palm trees in Devon, Great Britain, which is warmed by an ocean current

Current effects

Ocean currents affect the climate. For example, a warm current that starts near the equator gives western Europe a temperate climate although other places that are as far north have much colder climates.

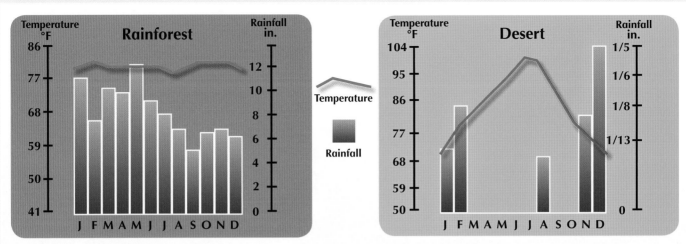

Temperature °F — Rainforest — Rainfall in.

Temperature °F — Desert — Rainfall in.

Temperature

Rainfall

Climographs

A climograph is a diagram showing rainfall and temperature throughout an average year. The climograph for a rainforest shows high rainfall and constant temperatures throughout the year. The climograph for a desert shows little, irregular rainfall and wide temperature range.

Europe

Asia

Africa

Australasia

A buffalo near the boundary between continental and temperate climate zones

Shifting zones

The edges of climate zones look clear on a map, but in reality they may overlap and even shift year by year. For example, in warm years, the edge of the north polar zone may shift to the north as the ice melts.

Local zones

Different climate zones may exist within the boundaries of other zones. For example, the tops of mountain ranges in a temperate zone will have a polar climate.

Antarctica

Biomes

A biome is a type of natural environment that covers a wide area. There are several different kinds of biomes, including deserts, grasslands, and rainforests. A biome includes not only the place itself, but also the plants and animals that live there.

What is a biome?

Biomes are partly determined by their geography, such as whether they are mountainous or flat, or contain rivers or oceans. Large biomes, which include wetlands, such as the Okavango Delta in Botswana, may include smaller biomes, such as rivers or woodland. Smaller biomes are sometimes called habitats. Climate is the main reason biomes of the world are different from each other. That is why biomes are often described by their climates, such as tropical forests or temperate grasslands.

Top Facts

- Some types of plants and animals can live in several different biomes. Others are found in only one kind.

- Plants and animals are often well adapted for life in a biome. For example, cactuses in desert biomes have fleshy stems that store water.

It's Amazing!

The world's largest coral reef is the Great Barrier Reef, off the coast of eastern Australia. It is 1,180 miles long.

Coral reefs

Coral polyps are tiny sea creatures that live in large groups. The hard covering they make for themselves forms coral reefs—a type of biome. Coral reefs are mainly found in tropical zones, where they attract a great variety of sea life.

Coral reef in the Red Sea off the coast of Egypt

Shaping biomes

Climate affects biomes by changing the landscape. For example, the cold climate means that polar biomes are covered in snow. Climate also affects what plants grow in a biome. For example, many large, green plants grow in rainforests because they get plenty of sun and water. The plants that grow in a biome determine which animals live there because the animals eat the plants or other animals that feed on the plants.

The Okavango Delta in Botswana, Africa

Cave climates

Caves, such as this one in France, are a type of habitat where the temperature is constant. This is because they are sheltered from sunlight and wind. Caves are usually cool and dark inside.

Artificial biomes

People can make artificial biomes by building special temperature-controlled structures that have their own climates. The Eden Project in Great Britain has huge domes made of transparent foil, and each dome holds a different biome. The Tropics biome (left) is the largest greenhouse in the world.

The domes at the Eden Project contain more than a million plants from around the world.

Polar climates

The Arctic, or North Pole, and Antarctica, or the South Pole, are the coldest places on the planet. Much of the Arctic is frozen ocean, and the continent of Antarctica is so cold that it is completely covered in ice. These are harsh biomes, where few types of plants and animals live.

Poles apart

Antarctica is a rocky continent covered in ice that is up to $2\frac{3}{4}$ miles thick. It is a high, mountainous land, where it is incredibly cold. The Arctic is mostly a huge sheet of sea ice floating on the Arctic Ocean. In winter, seawater cools down more slowly than land, which stops the temperature in the Arctic from dropping as low as it does in Antarctica.

Learn about blubber

- Polar animals, such as whales and seals, have a thick layer of fat called blubber. It keeps them warm in the icy waters.
- To see how this works, fill a rubber glove with some margarine.
- Put your hand inside and then place your hand in a bowl of very cold water.
- See how long you can keep your hand in the water before it feels cold.

Fastest winds

The climate of Antarctica is made more extreme by the fast, icy winds that blow across the continent. Cold, high-pressure air flows swiftly down the high, icy mountains in the middle of Antarctica. These winds are pushed away, or deflected, by Earth's rotation, creating super-fast winds that spiral out from the centre of the continent. The wind chill (see page 37) lowers the temperature by at least 18°F.

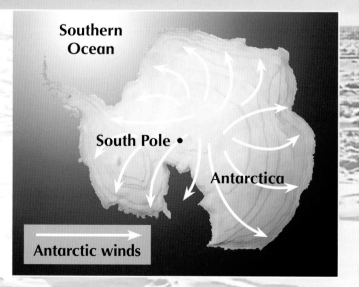

Southern Ocean

South Pole •

Antarctica

Antarctic winds

Where on Earth?

Antarctica is the fifth largest continent. It is about one-and-a-half times bigger than the United States. In winter, the ocean around it freezes and doubles the size of the continent. The Arctic is mainly made up of the Arctic Ocean, but it also includes thousands of islands and the northern parts of Europe, Asia, and North America.

The Arctic

North America

Europe

Asia

Africa

South America

Australasia

Antarctica

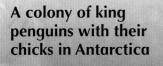

A colony of king penguins with their chicks in Antarctica

Cold and dry

The areas around the North and South poles are often described as cold deserts. This is because the water in polar regions is not in its liquid form, but is frozen into ice. In Antarctica, any snow that falls remains solid and never melts into liquid water. Plants cannot use ice to grow and animals cannot drink ice, so the polar regions are as barren as a hot desert.

Sea ice in the Arctic

Polar seasons

There are seasons at the poles. In winter, the Sun never rises and there is 24-hour darkness. In the brief summer, the Sun never sets and the temperature rises a little. Most Antarctic animals, such as king penguins, breed during the milder summer.

It's Amazing!

Most of the sunlight that hits the poles bounces back into the atmosphere because the white ice is reflective. Some parts of Antarctica reflect as much as 90 percent of the sunlight that hits this region, compared to a global average of 31 percent.

Cool climates

To the south of the Arctic is a large belt of treeless land called tundra. The climate is still cold there, but the region is free from snow and ice during the summer. South of the tundra is an enormous strip of a type of forest called taiga.

The tundra

In winter, the average temperature in the tundra is about -30°F. There is little rain, and harsh winds dry the land out even more. Tundra summers last only six to eight weeks, and they are too cold for trees to grow but lichens and mosses cover the land.

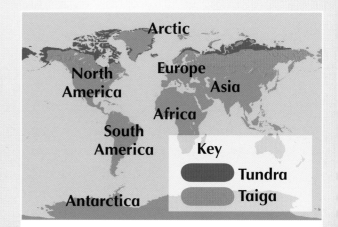

Arctic

North America

Europe

Asia

Africa

South America

Key

Tundra

Taiga

Antarctica

Where on Earth?

Tundra covers a wide area of land in the far north of Europe, Asia, and North America just south of the Arctic. Tundra is also found on the edge of Antarctica and in high mountain regions. The taiga forests are found next to the Arctic tundra, below the tree line—the point above which it is too cold for trees to grow.

Changing color

Many animals living in cold climates have adapted to conditions there in special ways. The Arctic fox, for example, can change the color of its coat. It grows a white coat in winter so it can hide from its prey in the snow. This coat molts in summer to reveal brown fur.

Biggest forests

Taiga forests cover one fifth of all the land on the planet, and they form the biggest land biome of all. Taiga forests are made up of conifer trees, such as pine, spruce, and fir. Their needlelike leaves have a waxy coating that helps to protect them from the snow and ice during the long winters. The short summers are warm and wet.

Taiga forest in North America

It's Amazing!

Lemmings are small Arctic rodents with fur on their feet. In winter, they grow long claws to help them dig tunnels under the tightly packed snow. The tunnels help protect the lemmings from the cold and any predators.

The top layer of soil thaws in summer.

Lake

Permafrost

Top Facts

- Climate causes animals to migrate, or travel long distances, to find food or to breed. For example, in spring, huge herds of reindeer migrate up to 5,000 miles to the tundra to breed.

- The temperature range in the taiga varies from about -58°F to about 86°F.

Permafrost

Permafrost is a layer of soil so cold that it remains frozen throughout the year. This layer lies just beneath the surface of the land and stretches from a few inches to 1,000 feet deep. Permafrost covers about one fifth of the world's land surface, including most of Alaska, northern Canada, and Siberia.

Temperate climates

Temperate climate zones lie halfway between the equator and the poles. Plants and animals in temperate zones have adapted to cope with the cool, wet winters and warm, dry summers.

Grass and trees

The two main biomes in temperate zones are forests and grasslands. Forests grow in the wetter parts of the temperate zones and grasslands grow in the drier areas. Most of the temperate forests are deciduous (the trees drop their leaves in winter), but some are evergreen (the trees keep their leaves all year).

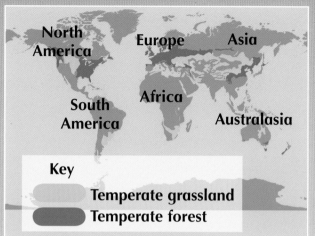

North America
Europe
Asia
South America
Africa
Australasia

Key
Temperate grassland
Temperate forest

Where on Earth?

Temperate deciduous forests are found in North America and Central Europe, as well as Asia, southern South America, and New Zealand. Temperate evergreen forests grow mostly in coastal South America. Temperate grasslands include the prairies of North America and the steppes of Russia.

A herd of deer graze on grasslands in Great Britain.

On the grass

Large animals that live on the temperate grasslands include wild horses, bison, antelopes, and deer. They gather in large groups called herds. Other grassland animals include prairie dogs, which live in burrows underground for safety.

Coping with change

Photosynthesis is the process green plants use to make food from air, water, and sunlight. In fall and winter, there is not enough sunlight in temperate zones for photosynthesis, so the leaves on deciduous trees, such as beech and oak, change color and fall off. The branches are bare until spring, when new leaves grow.

It's Amazing!

The largest living thing on the planet is a temperate giant redwood tree in California called General Sherman. It is as heavy as 14 blue whales!

Enormous trees

The warmest, wettest parts of the temperate zone are home to the tallest forests on the planet. For example, in the forest along the Pacific Coast of the United States, there are massive conifers. These giant evergreen trees can grow to more than 260 feet tall.

Top Facts

- The weight of a mature deciduous tree trunk is greater than the combined weight of the leaves, branches, and roots attached to it.

- In Argentina, South America, the temperate grasslands are called the pampas.

This area of countryside in Germany includes deciduous trees, evergreen trees, and grassland.

Tropical climates

Tropical climate zones are almost always hot and humid. These are ideal conditions for trees and other plants to grow all year. A great many animals live in the trees, eating the leaves and fruit.

Tropical forest

Tropical forests are often called rainforests. In the hot, tropical sun, water evaporates fast from the leaves—each tall tree can lose 200 gallons from its leaves. The warm, humid air rises and cools to form clouds that shade the forest from the strong sunlight.

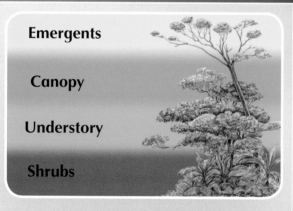

Emergents

Canopy

Understory

Shrubs

A gibbon swings in the trees of an Asian rainforest.

Forest layers

A rainforest has four layers. The canopy is formed of high branches. Tall trees, called emergents, stick out of the canopy. Below the canopy are the smaller trees of the understory, and on the forest floor there are shrubs.

Top Facts

- Rainforests cover about 6 percent of the land on the earth but are home to more than half of all plant and animal species.

- The savanna of Africa is home to the largest land animal, the African elephant, which can weigh up to $7\frac{3}{4}$ tons.

Savanna

Tropical grasslands are also called savannas. In these regions, there are distinct seasons—a long, hot dry season and a short rainy season with a lot of thunderstorms. Most of the land in a savanna is covered in grass, with some small clumps of shrubs and trees. The plants grow mainly in the rainy season. During the long dry season, the plants die back and turn brown and the ground becomes dusty and dry.

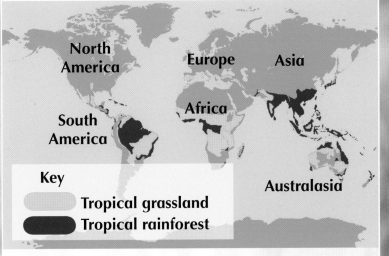

Key

Tropical grassland

Tropical rainforest

Where on Earth?

The tropical zone lies on either side of the equator. The biggest tropical forests are in South America, central Africa, and Southeast Asia. Tropical grasslands include the African savanna and the South American pampas.

Lionesses hunt on the savanna in Africa.

It's Amazing!

Dung beetles on the savanna eat animal dung and lay their eggs in it. They also bury the dung. Without these beetles, the tropical grasslands would be piled deep in dung!

Hunters and hunted

The grasses of the savanna provide food for enormous herds of grazing animals, such as zebra, antelope, and wildebeest. These grazing animals are hunted by savanna predators, such as cheetahs, hyenas, and lions.

A wildebeest grazes on the African grasslands.

Mediterranean climates

Mediterranean zones have wet winters and long, dry summers. This type of climate occurs around the Mediterranean Sea in Europe, as well as in parts of North America, Australia, and Africa.

Highs and lows

In winter, the average temperature in the Mediterranean zone is about 55 degrees Fahrenheit, and it rarely drops below freezing. In summer, the average temperature rises to 80 degrees, and there is little rainfall. Dry air from the equator brings the long periods of summer drought.

Pumas live in California, which has a Mediterranean climate.

Sun protection

Some Mediterranean plants, such as lavender, contain fragrant oils in their leaves. These evaporate in the heat to keep the plants cool. They also perfume the air.

Top Facts

- The long, dry summers of the Mediterranean zone in Europe have made it a popular tourist destination.

- Places with Mediterranean climates often have dry winds in summer. One of these winds is the sirocco in Italy, which blows from the Sahara.

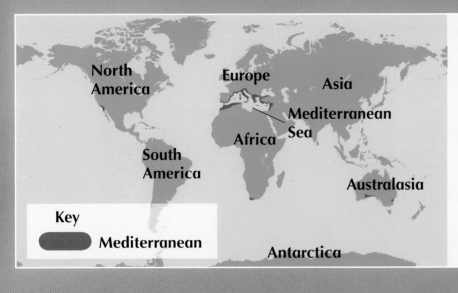

Where on Earth?

Mediterranean zones are not only found around the Mediterranean Sea. Other examples are the chapparal of California, mallee scrub of Australia, and fynbos of South Africa. Mediterranean climates are also found in parts of Chile and western Australia.

Plant life

Many Mediterranean plants have adapted to cope with the summer droughts. Some are slow-growing shrubs or small trees. Others, such as olive, eucalyptus, and scrub oak, have tough leaves or thick bark to help them survive the extreme heat and dryness of the summer months. Many plants have hairy leaves, which collect more moisture from the air than flat leaves do.

A scorpion paralyzes its prey with a stinger in its tail.

Scrub hunters

A great variety of animals live in the Mediterranean zones. There are wild rabbits, goats, and sheep, which are hunted by lynx, puma, vultures, and eagles. Many Mediterranean animals, such as scorpions, are nocturnal, which means they hide during the day to escape the heat and come out to feed at night.

It's Amazing!

Farmers from the Mediterranean often plant delicate orange and lemon trees on slopes. In spells of cold weather, the plants on the slopes are more likely to escape frost damage because cold air sinks to the bottom of the valleys.

Hot desert climates

A region must have less than 6 inches of rainfall a year to be classified as a desert. Hot deserts are extreme landscapes where strong sunshine scorches the land in the day but the nights are extremely cold.

Red Rock Canyon in Nevada is part of the Mojave Desert.

Golden sand dunes in the Sahara, Africa

Sand and rock

Most of the world's deserts are rocky and covered in small boulders and stones. There is no soil in deserts because soil is made up of rotted plant and animal matter, as well as tiny pieces of rock. As desert climates are too hot and dry for many plants to grow, there is not enough plant waste to form soil.

Top Facts

- The world's largest hot desert is the Sahara. It covers more than 3¼ million square miles. It is almost as large as the United States.

- Deserts cover about one fifth of the planet's land surface.

- Some deserts are so hot that animals hide below ground during the day and come out only at night.

The dryness of deserts

Many deserts are found near the tropics of Cancer and Capricorn, where it is hot and dry and far from the oceans. Deserts also form in rain shadows (see page 40). In some places, the small amount of rain that falls takes the form of heavy showers once every few years. Torrential rain can cause flash floods, with rushing waters that change the landscape. Other deserts have rain more often, but it is light and evaporates quickly because of the heat.

Where on Earth?

Hot desert biomes with sand dunes and almost no plants are found in North Africa, the Middle East, and parts of central Australia. Rocky semideserts have a few more plants because rainfall is more regular, although still low. These include the Kalahari in southern Africa and the Mojave in the United States.

Mojave

Gobi

Sahara

Arabian

Namib

Atacama

Kalahari

Australian

Key

Deserts

It's Amazing!

In the deserts of North Africa, the temperature can be as high as 99.5 degrees Farenheit in the daytime, but drop to 33 degrees Farenheit at night!

Saving water

Plants have developed several ways of surviving in deserts. Some have seeds that stay dormant, or rest, beneath the ground for a long time until there is enough rain for them to grow. Cactuses have shallow, widely spread roots to seek out water, which they store in their fleshy stems. They also have spines to stop animals eating them and stealing their water!

Hot and cold

Deserts get incredibly hot during the day because, with little water vapor in the air, no clouds form to stop the sunlight from reaching the ground. At night, the lack of clouds in the sky means that any heat is lost quickly, making deserts extremely cold.

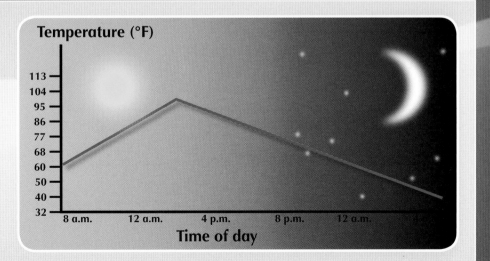

Temperature (°F)

113
104
95
86
77
68
60
50
40
32

8 a.m.　12 a.m.　4 p.m.　8 p.m.　12 a.m.

Time of day

Changing climates

The world's climate has not always been as it is today. Over many millions of years, it has slowly changed. In the past, climate change was due to natural events, but today it may be caused by people polluting the planet.

Past climates

Scientists use different kinds of evidence to study climate change. For example, fossils from the Sahara show that this region once had a cooler, wetter climate with crocodiles swimming in rivers. Rocks also provide evidence of past conditions in an area. For example, coal is a type of rock that formed millions of years ago in tropical swamps.

Eruption of Mount St. Helens, Washington, May 18, 1980

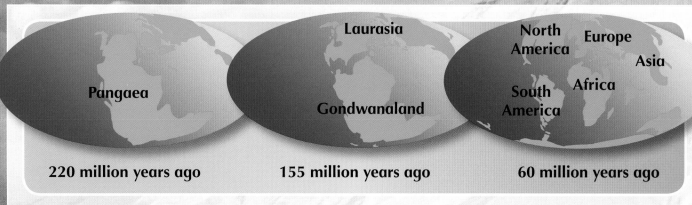

Pangaea

220 million years ago

Laurasia

Gondwanaland

155 million years ago

North America
Europe
Asia
Africa
South America

60 million years ago

Moving continents

About 220 million years ago, the continents were locked together in a giant landmass we call Pangaea. Then they drifted apart as large sections of the planet's crust shifted. About 155 million years ago, there were two continents, Laurasia and Gondwanaland. These slowly split until about 60 million years ago, when they began to form the continents we know today. The shifting continents meant that some places with hot climates moved to colder climates and vice versa.

Causes of climate change

Natural events, such as volcanic eruptions that block out sunlight, can temporarily change the climate. Today, scientists believe that many human activities, such as burning oil and other fossil fuels, are changing the climate forever.

Cloud of volcanic gas, ash, and dust

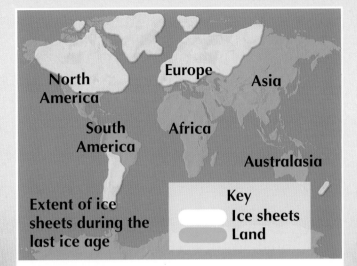

Ice ages

The most significant climate changes in the past were the ice ages. During the ice ages, the climate became so cold that temperate areas, such as northern Europe and North America, were covered by giant ice sheets. The last ice age began about 1.8 million years ago and ended about 11,000 years ago.

Extent of ice sheets during the last ice age

North America
Europe
Asia
South America
Africa
Australasia

Key
Ice sheets
Land

Top Facts

- Our planet's climate has changed many times since the planet formed 5 billion years ago.

- Our planet had a much warmer climate about 6,000 years ago, when the temperature was about 3.6°F higher than it is today.

Circles of irrigated land in the deserts of the southwestern United States

Desertification

Desertification is when an area of once-fertile land becomes dry and no good for growing crops. This can be caused by a change in the climate or by poor farming practices. Some countries have tried to stop the spread of deserts by irrigating, or watering, areas of land so that crops will grow there.

SEASONS

In some places, the weather is the same throughout the year. If you visited these regions, you could wear the same kind of clothes almost every single day. In other parts of the world, the weather changes during the year. Each different period of weather is called a season. For example, in some regions, there are hot, dry summers and cold, icy winters. But have you ever wondered what causes the changing seasons?

What causes the seasons?

Earth takes 365¼ days—one year—to orbit the Sun. Different parts of the world receive different amounts of sunlight throughout the year, and these variations cause the seasons.

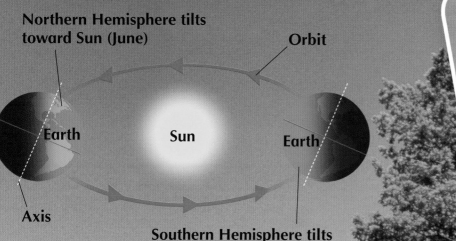

Northern Hemisphere tilts toward Sun (June)

Orbit

Earth

Sun

Earth

Axis

Southern Hemisphere tilts toward Sun (December)

How seasons happen

Earth's axis is tilted at an angle of 23.5 degrees to the Sun. This means that different parts of the planet are closer to the Sun at different times of the year. For example, from March to August, the Northern Hemisphere is closer to the Sun and has spring and summer seasons.

Earth may have been hit by a planet the size of Mars.

Why is Earth tilted?

No one knows for sure why Earth's axis is tilted. One idea is that the planet was struck by a large planet, which tipped Earth from a vertical position about 5 billion years ago. If the planet did not tilt, countries near the poles would be cold and dark all year round.

Seasonal lag

The hottest day of the year is about a month after the day when Earth is tilted most toward the Sun. This delay is called seasonal lag. It occurs because water vapor and gases in the atmosphere absorb some heat and slow down the speed at which the surface heats up.

Snow falls in New York City in February.

Seasonal gods

The ancient Greeks thought that their gods caused the seasons. Persephone was the daughter of the goddess of the harvest, Demeter. The Greeks thought fields grew cold and lifeless for several months over winter because Demeter was unhappy at Persephone's marriage to Hades, god of the underworld.

Opposite seasons

The tilt of the Earth means that the different hemispheres, or halves of the planet, have different seasons at the same time of the year. For instance, December to February is winter in the Northern Hemisphere but summer in the Southern Hemisphere. In March, the weather cools down in the Southern Hemisphere but starts to warm up in the Northern Hemisphere as it moves toward summer.

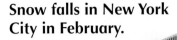
Ears of wheat ripen in the summer sunshine.

Long summer days

The long hours of sunlight during the summer are the best time for crops to grow and ripen. In the winter, the days are shorter and the sun appears lower in the sky. Few plants grow during these cold, dark winter days.

Measuring seasons

Different places around the world have different seasons. In some regions, the seasons are marked mainly by temperature differences. In others, the seasons depend on the amount of rainfall.

Four seasons

Temperate and polar climate zones have four seasons. In temperate zones, spring, summer, fall, and winter each last about three months. The days are longer during summer than during winter. In polar zones, there may be just a couple of hours of sunlight each day in midwinter.

Seasonal dates

In the past, people in Europe marked the change of the seasons about a month earlier than they do today. For example, spring began on February 2 and fall at the start of August. The ancient Romans changed the season dates to those most people in temperate areas use today when they conquered large parts of Europe about 2,000 years ago.

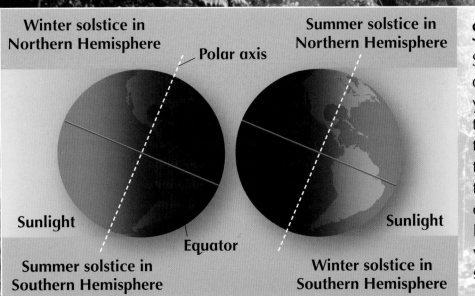

Winter solstice in Northern Hemisphere

Polar axis

Summer solstice in Northern Hemisphere

Sunlight

Sunlight

Equator

Summer solstice in Southern Hemisphere

Winter solstice in Southern Hemisphere

Solstices

Solstices are the longest and shortest days of the year. The summer solstice in the Northern Hemisphere is the day on which that half of the planet tilts most toward the Sun. It is the longest day of the year. In the Southern Hemisphere, this is the winter solstice and it is the shortest day of the year.

Two or three seasons

The major seasonal difference in tropical climate zones is in rainfall, not temperature, so the seasons are called wet and dry. They are not always the same length. Sometimes, all the year's rainfall comes in a wet season lasting about three months. The dry season is sometimes divided up into a cool part after the rain and a warm, more humid, part before the wet season begins again.

It's Amazing!

The Yolngu people of northern Australia named the "Burrugumiri" season after fish. This was when the water was warm enough for sharks and stingrays to have babies, which are called "burrugu."

North Pole

Equator

Sunlight

South Pole

Equinoxes

At certain points in Earth's orbit, neither hemisphere is tilted toward to the Sun more than the other. These are the "equinoxes," which means "equal night." They are the two days in the year when day and night are of equal length. These days fall on or around March 21 and September 23, or halfway between the summer and winter solstices.

Different seasons

Australia, in the Southern Hemisphere, has different seasons in different parts of the country. The north has a tropical climate with equal-length dry and wet seasons. The center and south have four seasons. There, Christmas falls during the hot summer and the cool winter is from June to August.

Australians celebrate Christmas in hot summer weather.

Buffalo have a thick coat of hair to protect them from the cold and snow.

Winter

In winter, the days are short and cold. There are often high winds, and sometimes snow covers the ground. When it gets really cold, frost may form on windows and ponds may freeze over.

Cold season

During the winter months, the sun does not appear high in the sky and the days are much shorter. As a result, less of the Sun's energy reaches the planet's surface in regions where it is winter, which is why winter temperatures are much colder than summer ones.

Moisture and cold air

Winter's low temperatures make water vapor in the clouds condense, or become liquid, quickly. The liquid may then freeze, forming snowflakes. Snow falls when the air below the clouds is cold, but it melts into sleet when the air is warmer.

Winter chill

Sinking cold air pushes air below out of the way, creating winds. Wind chill makes temperatures seem even colder. Animals feel the cold because the wind makes moisture on their skin evaporate, removing their body heat. The faster the wind blows, the greater the wind chill.

Wind speed (mph)	Exposed flesh will freeze in 30 seconds.						Frostbite likely					Frostbite possible		Very cold		Cold	
45	-108	-101	-94	-85	-78	-71	-62	-56	-47	-38	-31	-24	-15	-8	-1	9	17
40	-107	-99	-92	-83	-76	-69	-60	-54	-45	-36	-29	-22	-13	-6	3	10	18
35	-105	-99	-92	-83	-74	-67	-58	-53	-44	-35	-27	-20	-11	-4	5	10	19
30	-101	-94	-87	-80	-71	-64	-56	-49	-42	-33	-26	-18	-9	-2	7	12	21
25	-96	-89	-81	-74	-65	-60	-51	-44	-36	-29	-22	-15	-6	1	9	16	23
20	-89	-81	-74	-67	-60	-53	-45	-38	-31	-24	-17	-9	-2	3	12	19	27
15	-80	-72	-65	-58	-51	-42	-38	-31	-26	-18	-11	-6	1	9	16	23	28
10	-63	-60	-53	-45	-40	-35	-27	-22	-15	-9	-2	3	10	16	21	28	34
5	-42	-35	-31	-26	-20	-15	-9	-6	0	7	10	16	21	27	32	37	43
	-35	-30	-25	-20	-15	-10	-5	0	5	10	15	20	25	30	35	40	45

Air temperature (°F)

Plants in winter

To survive the cold and lack of light, plants undergo several changes in the winter. Deciduous trees grow buds on their bare branches to protect new leaves that will emerge in spring. Some plants, such as sunflowers, die. Others, such as daffodils, survive as bulbs underground, where temperatures are not as cold as in the air.

It's Amazing!

Diamond dust is the name given to a type of cloud that sinks to the ground and freezes. Water vapor turns directly into tiny ice crystals that glitter like diamonds in the sunlight.

Top Facts

- When animals hibernate, their body rates slow and their temperatures drop. The temperature of a ground squirrel will drop to as low as 28 degrees Farenheit.

- In contrast, a bear's body temperature will only drop to 88 degrees Farenheit, and scientists say that it does not truly hibernate.

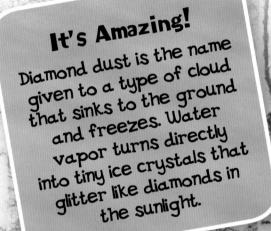

Some animals, such as dormice, spend the winter in a deep sleep called hibernation.

Keeping warm

Animals have different ways of keeping warm in winter. Birds may grow thicker layers of feathers. Some animals, such as mice, build nests in holes. They line these with feathers, moss, and fur to create a layer of insulation that keeps them warm.

A meadow saffron germinates.

Germination

In spring, frozen ground thaws and rain wets the soil. Seeds that have been inactive in the soil all winter take in water and swell. This triggers the growth of roots and shoots—germination.

Spring

In spring, the Earth starts to tilt back toward the Sun, bringing warmer weather. Snow and ice thaw, days get longer, and temperatures rise. Plants begin to grow again, and animals return or emerge from hibernation.

Birds, such as this chaffinch, and other animals become more active in the spring.

Test germination

- Most seeds need water and heat to germinate.
- Test this by sowing four runner bean seeds in pots of potting mix. Wet the soil in two pots. Then, put one wet and one dry pot in a dark refrigerator and one wet pot and one dry pot on a warm, light windowsill.
- Which seed germinates first? Do you know why?

Spring weather

Spring is the season between winter and summer. There are some warm days but some cold ones, too. Spring is generally wetter than the other seasons. Temperatures become high enough to evaporate more surface water than in winter. Cold and warm air masses meet up, creating winds that blow rain around in gusts.

Flowers bloom on a woodland floor in spring.

New growth

Rising temperatures and longer days trigger new growth in plants. Buds on trees and shrubs swell and open, revealing leaves inside. At first shrivelled, the leaves expand to their full size after sucking up rainwater through the plant's roots. Leaves also grow from bulbs underground and poke through the soil. The new plant growth provides a lot of food for animals.

Flowers in spring

Temperate woodland plants, such as scilla and cyclamen, use the spring sunshine to grow leaves and flowers rapidly before the trees above them are fully in leaf. If these plants blossomed any later, the leaves on the trees would block the heat and light they need to grow.

Pollination

Seeds form when pollen grains from one plant reach other flowers from the same species. Insects, such as bumblebees, pick up and carry the pollen when they visit flowers to feed. Some plants, such as willow trees, rely on spring winds to blow their pollen from tree to tree.

Pollen grains seen under a powerful microscope

Summer

Summer is the season with the longest, warmest, and driest days. Skies are often blue and free from clouds, and sunlight is bright and strong. People usually spend more time outside, on beaches, in parks, and in gardens, enjoying the good weather.

Summer heat

In the summer, places are tilted toward the Sun. The heat warms up the air. Because warm air is less dense than cool air, it rises and creates areas of low pressure. The air is still on summer days because there are only low-pressure air masses in the sky above. Precipitation comes in short, heavy bursts, and the air is often humid because the warmth evaporates a lot of water.

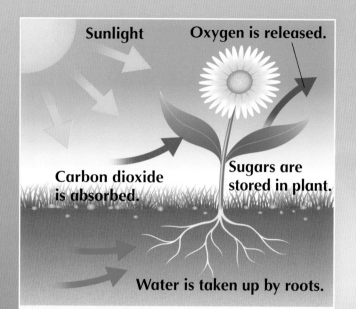

Sunlight

Oxygen is released.

Carbon dioxide is absorbed.

Sugars are stored in plant.

Water is taken up by roots.

How plants make food

Plants use energy from sunlight to change carbon dioxide gas from the air, and water from the soil, into sugar. This process is called photosynthesis. It is carried out in a substance called chlorophyll inside leaves. Plants turn some sugar into energy for growth and repair, but most into starch, which they store for later use. They also release oxygen into the air.

A summer's day in Central Park, New York City

It's Amazing!

People feel cooler wearing light colors in summer. This is because heat bounces off light colors, but is absorbed by dark colors!

Harvesting a crop that has ripened in the summer

Growing time

Crops such as wheat and beans grow fastest in the heat of early summer. Their roots suck up water from the drying soil. In late summer, the driest time of the year, farmers often irrigate, or water, crops to stop them from wilting and even dying.

Top Facts

- Summer nights are mild because water vapor in the air that has evaporated from plant leaves traps daytime heat.

- The temperature range in summer is usually less than in spring or fall. This is because, although daytime temperatures are higher, nighttime temperatures are much higher, too.

Keeping cool

In warm summer weather, our bodies need to adjust to the higher temperatures. For example, blood vessels just beneath the skin expand, so that heat from our blood escapes into the air, helping to cool us down.

Sun-ripened fruit

Many plants produce fruit, such as tomatoes, in summer. The fruit protect seeds, which are developing inside them. The fruit changes color and produces a strong smell to attract animals, such as birds. These animals then spread the seeds around as they eat the fruit.

Fall

The shorter, wetter days and longer, colder nights of fall bring many changes after the hot calm of summer. Leaves change color and drop off some trees. Animals start to gather and store food ready for the winter.

Weather changes

Earth starts to tilt away from the Sun in fall, so there is less heat and light. Temperature differences start to increase and the weather becomes wetter and windier as we move toward winter.

Oak leaves turn brown.

Fall leaves

There is not enough sunlight in fall for trees and other plants to make much food by photosynthesis, so they start to live on their stored food. In broad-leaved trees, such as the oak, winds cause leaves to lose water and low temperatures damage them, so these trees drop all their leaves.

Litter life

The blanket of fallen leaves, or leaf litter, beneath plants in fall provides food and shelter for many living things. Creatures such as millipedes and worms break the leaves down into little pieces, and fungi and bacteria break the pieces down even further, releasing nutrients. The nutrients mix into the soil, making it rich and fertile for the new growing season.

A toadstool is a kind of fungus.

Why leaves change color

Leaves are green because the chlorophyll inside them is green, but there are also yellow and orange chemicals inside leaves. When tree leaves start to die, the chlorophyll disappears, leaving the other colors. Chemical changes in leaves can create different colors, such as red, brown, yellow, or even purple. Evergreen plants, such as conifer trees, have tough, waxy leaves that survive cold temperatures and prevent water loss. Their leaves do not drop in fall.

Leaves turn brown in a forest in New England during fall.

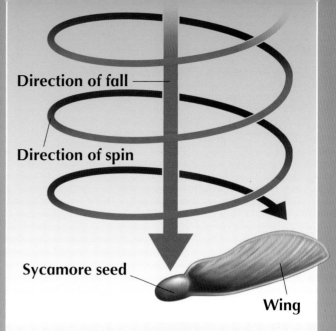

Direction of fall

Direction of spin

Sycamore seed

Wing

Spreading seeds

Many plants spread their seeds in fall. Sycamore trees spread their seeds in wing-shaped cases that spin as they fall from trees, carrying the seeds far from the parent tree. This gives them more chance to germinate. Some trees, such as hazel and apple trees, cover their seeds in nuts and fruit. The seeds are then spread when animals eat or store the nuts and fruit.

It's Amazing!

A single oak tree makes as many as 2,200 acorns, but an average of only one out of every 10,000 acorns will grow into a new oak tree!

Leaf litter critters

- Fill a funnel with leaf litter and place it over a jar painted black and lined with a damp paper towel.
- Shine a lamp down into the funnel. Creatures in the litter will try to escape the light by falling into the jar, where you can study them.
- Make sure you return the creatures when you have finished the experiment.

Animal life cycles

Animal life cycles, or the changes from young to adult, usually follow the seasons. Wild animals need the right weather so that there are enough plants to provide them with food and shelter when they are trying to raise their young.

Spring and summer

The spring growth of plants provides food for many different animals. This increase in food gives animals the chance to give birth to and feed young babies. For instance, bees carry pollen from flowers to their nests for their young to eat. Throughout the summer there is even more food for the young animals to eat. This means that they can grow big and strong enough to survive the coming winter.

A blue tit feeds its young.

Tree tales

A single tree may be home to many different animals through the seasons. For example, moths lay eggs on oak leaves. Caterpillars hatch from these eggs and feed on the leaves. Birds nesting in the tree feed on the juicy caterpillars.

Test your memory

- Squirrels store thousands of nuts in fall and can remember where half of them are in the winter.
- Test your own memory by burying ten stones in a sandbox. Smooth the sand over each hole and leave them overnight. Can you remember where you put them all?

Prairie dogs emerge from their burrow in spring after hibernating, or sleeping, through the winter.

Fall and winter

In fall, some animals, such as rabbits, grow thick hair to keep warm in the coming cold weather. Birds and squirrels eat large amounts of fruit and nuts to gain weight so they can survive when there is less food available in winter. Then, when the weather warms up in spring and plants begin to grow, the animals prepare to have young and start the yearly cycle again.

A squirrel checks on its store of nuts.

Hoarding

Many animals hoard, or store, food to last them through the winter. Squirrels, for example, bury nuts one at a time in the ground or in groups in hollow trees. Acorn woodpeckers peck holes in dead trees and push acorns inside.

It's Amazing!

Squirrels are clever hoarders. They sometimes pretend to bury nuts. This is to confuse birds, such as jays, that try to steal the buried nuts.

Grass   Reindeer   Wolf

Food chains

A food chain is a way of showing what animals eat and what eats them. It always starts with a plant, which makes its own food, and ends with an animal that is rarely eaten by other animals itself. In the example above, grass is eaten by a reindeer, which is eaten by a pack of wolves. The new plant growth in spring starts off many different food chains.

Stay or leave?

Many animals live in places where the changing seasons bring a severe shortage of food or extreme temperatures. Some of these animals choose to stay and survive the conditions, for example, by hibernating. Others migrate, which means making a long journey to somewhere with better weather.

Hibernation

Hibernation is a deep sleep some animals use to survive cold winters. Animals that hibernate include bats, toads, groundhogs, and ladybugs. During hibernation, their body temperature cools, they breathe slowly and their heart almost stops beating. This helps them survive without eating in low temperatures. Some animals, such as hedgehogs, eat a lot of food to fatten up before hibernating.

Top Facts

- A bat's heart normally beats about 400 times per minute. When a bat hibernates, the heart beats only 15 or 20 times per minute. This saves 99 percent of the energy the bat would normally use.

- Some animals wake from hibernation to urinate because otherwise the waste products in the urine could poison them.

A hibernating hedgehog

A warm place

Hibernating animals keep a near constant body temperature by finding sheltered places to stay. In autumn, hedgehogs collect piles of dry leaves. When winter begins, they curl up into a ball under the leaves and wait for the spring.

Swallows rest on telephone lines during their migration.

Migration

Animals migrate to escape extreme cold or heat, to find places with more food or to mate. Migrating animals include butterflies, salmon, whales, reindeer, and birds. Each spring, swallows fly about 6,000 miles from Africa to Europe. They do this because it is too hot in Africa to rear their young. In September, the swallows start their six-week journey back.

It's Amazing!

The Arctic tern travels around the Earth each year to have two summers! It breeds in the Arctic tundra in the Northern Hemisphere summer. It then flies south to spend the Southern Hemisphere summer in Antarctica.

Snails gather under a shady leaf to sleep.

Heat sleep

Some animals use a kind of sleep called aestivation to survive the heat. Land snails seal themselves into their shells with dried slime. They rest in this condition until the dry weather ends.

Migration and weather

Clouds, winds, and storms cause big problems for some migrating animals. Tired land birds, such as warblers for example, may be blown out to sea where they cannot find food or places to stop and rest. Some birds are able to fly high and rise above any bad weather. They can also make use of the fast currents of air called jet streams (see page 30).

Snow geese migrate south during the winter.

Wet and dry seasons

In regions on or near the equator, water evaporates quickly in the heat, forming a belt of cloud. As Earth tilts toward and away from the Sun, this belt of cloud shifts north and south, causing rainy and dry seasons.

Hot, dry months

The hottest part of the dry season transforms the land. The baked earth cracks and lush grasses turn brown. The amount of water in rivers and lakes drops. Fish die, and other animals go hungry and thirsty.

A boy in Cambodia leads his cow along a dried-up river during the dry season.

Tropical seasons

The tropics are the regions between two imaginary lines around the globe at 23 degrees north and 23 degrees south of the equator (see map on page 81). From October to March, there is a rainy season in the southern tropics and a dry season in the northern tropics. The seasons swap from April to September.

Keeping cool

Animals find different ways to keep cool in the tropical heat. Many, such as lions, find shade under trees and bushes. Others, such as elephants, wallow in mud or coat themselves in dust.

A pair of lions in Kenya shelter in the shade to escape the heat of the sun.

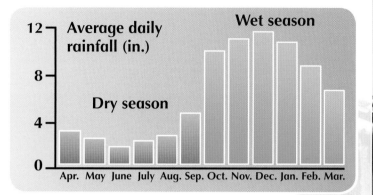

Annual rainfall in a tropical region

Average daily rainfall (in.)

Wet season

Dry season

12

8

4

0

Apr. May June July Aug. Sep. Oct. Nov. Dec. Jan. Feb. Mar.

Wet and dry

In the rainy season, most days start off hot and sunny. Humidity builds during the day, and a dip in temperature in the afternoon triggers rain. There may be up to 12 inches of rainfall each day. In the dry season, by contrast, rainfall may be just an inch or two or even zero.

A flooded family home in Vietnam during the wet season

Between the seasons

There is rarely a sudden change from dry to rainy seasons. The earliest part of the dry season is quite humid because a lot of water evaporates from the wet soil and plants. As the dry season progresses, no rain falls and the air dries. Toward the end of the dry season, however, the air starts to become humid again. Eventually, there is enough moisture in the air for clouds to form and for rain to fall and start the wet season.

Top Facts

- The length of the wet and dry seasons depends on how close a place is to the sea and on its altitude.

- There is often thunder and lightning in the rainy season because hot air masses over land clash with cooler, humid air blowing in from the oceans.

Extreme seasons

The farther north or south you live in the world, the more extreme the seasons are. At the polar zones, seasons range from months of cold darkness to milder weeks of constant sunlight. In many places on the equator, the weather is the same all year.

Polar circles

The Arctic Circle is the area in the Northern Hemisphere that surrounds the North Pole. It marks the limit of the region that experiences continuous dark in winter and continuous day in summer. Similarly, the Antarctic Circle marks the limit of the region around the South Pole that has continuous dark in winter and light in summer.

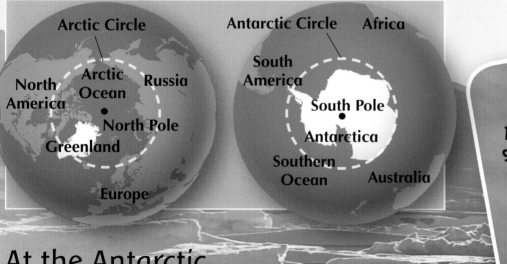

Arctic Circle

North America

Arctic Ocean

Russia

North Pole

Greenland

Europe

Antarctic Circle

Africa

South America

South Pole

Antarctica

Southern Ocean

Australia

At the Antarctic

The seven-month Antarctic winter is dark and very cold. Ice forms on the ocean around the continent. Summers are warmer, so the sea ice disappears. Antarctic land is far too cold and has too little food for many animals to live there. The few that do include penguins and elephant seals, which feed on fish in the milder Southern Ocean, and spend time on land only in summer.

Top Facts

- Most of the planet at the equator is covered in ocean, apart from areas of South America, Central Africa, and Indonesia.

- Only 4 inches of snow fall on Antarctica each year, so it is a frozen desert. Temperatures can fall as low as -130°F, which also makes it the coldest place on the planet.

It's Amazing!

Antarctica contains 90 percent of all our planet's ice. If all the ice there suddenly melted, sea levels around the world would rise by 200 feet!

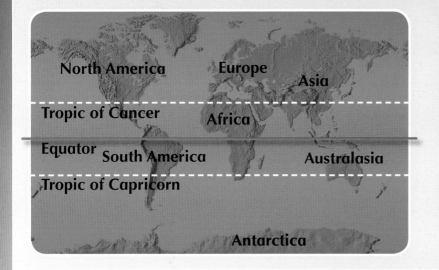

Equatorial weather

On the equator, the sun rises and sets in just a few minutes. The climate is so similar all year round that many people say there are no seasons at the equator. North and south of the equator are the tropics. These mark the points when the Sun is directly overhead at the summer and winter solstices (see page 64).

Arctic seasons

Most of the Arctic, including the North Pole and the ice sheet over the Arctic Ocean, is dry with extremely cold winters and milder summers. Some Arctic lands are wetter, with more snow and even rain. Winter is completely dark for five months. Fall and spring last only about a month each. In summer, there is enough warmth for some areas of frozen ground to thaw.

A team of huskies are driven over the Arctic ice.

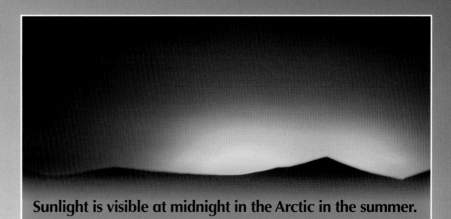

Sunlight is visible at midnight in the Arctic in the summer.

Land of the midnight sun

For almost ten weeks during summer, the Sun's rays hit the surface of the Arctic all the time. From the ground, the sun remains above the horizon for 24 hours a day and appears to make a circle around the sky without setting.

Special seasons

Some weather-related events happen regularly each year, and are also known as seasons. In certain places, wildfires rage across vast areas of forest when the weather is hot and dry. In other areas, huge storms, known as hurricanes, roll in from the ocean, bringing devastating winds and rain.

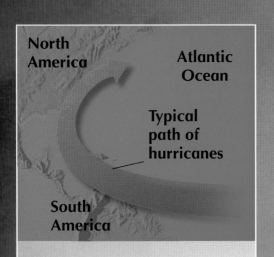

North America
Atlantic Ocean
Typical path of hurricanes
South America

Hurricane path

In the Northern Hemisphere, hurricanes move west or north from the central Atlantic Ocean. As they travel, their power is fueled by water evaporating from the warm ocean, creating rising currents of air.

Hurricane seasons

Hurricanes are among the most violent storms on the planet (see pages 102–103). The hurricane season in the Caribbean Sea occurs from May to October, but it is a month later in the cooler north Atlantic and Pacific waters because they take longer to warm up. The worst hurricanes usually happen in September.

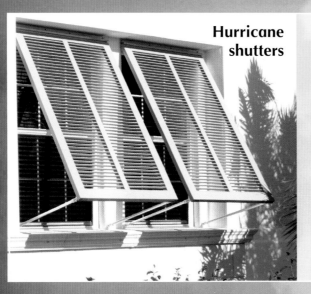

Hurricane shutters

Hurricane preparation

People prepare for the hurricane season each year. They make their houses strong enough to survive the storms—for example, by putting shutters on windows. They also prepare to leave their homes to go to safer places, following evacuation routes (see page 194). People watch the news and wait for instructions on when to leave.

Firefighters watch a prescribed burn in Utah.

Tackling a blaze

Firefighters tackle wildfires by spraying on water and special chemicals that stop fires from burning. They also clear paths in the forest, cutting down trees so there is no wood for the fire to burn. They might even light a fire to stop wildfires spreading! This is called a prescribed burn, and it clears away any dry undergrowth and plants that may burn easily and help to spread a wildfire.

Wildfire seasons

Wildfires are uncontrolled fires that start in very dry weather, when trees and other plants burn most easily. Some are started by lightning strikes, while others are started by people lighting small campfires. They happen in temperate and tropical climates. Wildfires are most destructive when they are fanned by strong winds, and they can destroy large areas of forest and vegetation very quickly.

Firefighters tackle a blaze in California.

It's Amazing!

The 2005 hurricane season was the worst on record, with 15 hurricanes. Seven of these were extremely powerful and damaging. For example, the winds in Hurricane Wilma blew at 185 miles per hour!

Top Facts

- The wildfire season is June to August in some western American states, such as Colorado and Arizona, and October to January in parts of Australia, such as Queensland and New South Wales.

- Hurricanes bring intense rainfall that creates floods, mud slides, and other events, which cause damage after the winds have dropped.

Celebrating seasons

People often celebrate the arrival of new seasons because of the change in weather. For example, spring brings weather suitable for sowing seeds and the end of summer is the time for harvesting crops.

Welcoming spring and summer

It is no surprise that people from many different places celebrate the coming of spring and summer—especially before the invention of heating systems and electric light—because winter can be cold, dark, and miserable. In Scandinavia, for example, people celebrate the arrival of the summer solstice (see page 64) with dancing, bonfires, and traditional food.

Harvest festivals

Harvest festivals are a way of celebrating the harvest, the time when farmers gather in their crops. Harvest festivals are usually celebrated with a big meal because this is a time of plenty, when the warmth of summer has ripened wheat and other crops.

Thanksgiving

Early settlers from Great Britain took the idea of harvest festivals to North America. This is the origin of the Thanksgiving festival, which was first celebrated by the Pilgrims in 1621 to give thanks for a successful harvest. It is now a national holiday in the United States on the fourth Thursday in November every year.

It's Amazing!

The word harvest comes from the old English word "haerfest," meaning autumn, or fall.

Mexican equinox

Long ago in Mexico, the Mayan people built the Chichen Itza temple so that, during the equinox, sunlight creates a shadow that moves like a slithering snake. It was called the "descent of the serpent Kukulkan," and was seen as a sign of a good harvest. Today, many people still visit the temple to see this.

Mayan temple at Chichen Itza

Rain dances

Today, rain dances are celebrations of the arrival of the rainy season and the end of the hot, dry weather. In the past, however, rain dances were performed in the belief that they would bring rain and ensure the success of the harvest. Many Native Americans still perform the ritual today. These celebrations are a reminder of how important rain is to people all over the world, but especially to those in places with hot, dry seasons.

Dancers perform the Dragon dance during the Chinese New Year.

The Japanese celebrate the coming of spring with "hanami" parties, where they picnic under flowering cherry blossom trees.

Chinese New Year

Chinese New Year marks the end of winter. It usually starts about a month after Christmas. This day falls on a different date each year, between January 21 and February 20, and is a time of great celebration.

WILD WEATHER

The wild weather that hits our planet every year can vary greatly. It can include winds that race across the land as fast as a train, snowfall so heavy that people cannot tell where the ground stops and the sky begins, and lightning flashes that light up the sky in the middle of the night. Although extreme weather can be exciting, it can also be dangerous and leave devastation in its path.

Extreme weather

Most of the time, the weather systems that move through the atmosphere produce moderate changes in weather. Sometimes, however, the energy in these systems can build up to create powerful storms.

Where in the world

Some extreme weather, such as lightning, happens all over the planet. Other types, such as tornadoes and floods, can happen anywhere but are at their most destructive in particular places. Some weather, such as blizzards, can happen only in particularly cold places on the planet.

Deadly weather

Extreme weather kills and injures thousands of people each year and leaves many more homeless. The cost of mending, rebuilding, or replacing damaged property is immense. In 2005, the cost worldwide was a staggering 200 billion dollars.

A car crushed by a tree following a storm in Great Britain

Chasing storms

It is fascinating to witness the power of extreme weather. Storm chasers try to work out where powerful storms, such as tornadoes, will form. They may drive long distances following tornadoes, taking photos and film to record and try to learn more about them. Others fly planes into the center of raging storms to monitor wind patterns and speeds in their core.

Storm chasers watch an approaching thunderstorm in Kansas.

A tree damaged by lightning

Storm safety

Lightning is much hotter than the surface of the Sun and can burn or kill people. It usually strikes tall objects, such as trees and poles, especially if they are made of metal. In lightning storms, you should avoid wide open spaces and never shelter under trees.

Weather on other planets

Other planets in our solar system have even wilder weather! Venus is cloaked in thick clouds that trap heat from the Sun, giving an average temperature of 850°F! Pluto is so far from the Sun that it is four times colder than Antarctica. Winds on Mars produce dust storms so large that they cover the entire planet.

The planet Mars, where temperatures can sink to -200°F

Thunder and lightning

Thunder and lightning storms come from mighty cumulonimbus clouds. These storms also bring heavy rain. Lighting is a powerful discharge of electricity that can cause enormous damage to trees, buildings, and people.

Electrical clouds

Rising and sinking air currents in storm clouds toss around the ice crystals and raindrops in them, causing them to bump into each other. This rubbing creates a buildup of static electricity, which is an electrical charge caused by friction. The top of the cloud will have a positive electrical charge and the lower part of the cloud will have a negative electrical charge.

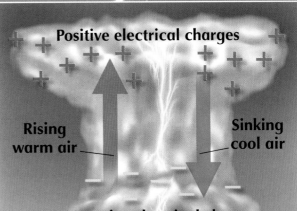

Positive electrical charges

Rising warm air

Sinking cool air

Negative electrical charges

Lightning

Positive electrical charges

Lightning flashes

As the air currents in the storm cloud swirl around, the electrical charges build up. Eventually, the difference between the negative charge in the cloud and the positive charge on the ground or at the top of the cloud becomes too great, and a powerful bolt of lightning leaps between them to equal out this difference.

Make lightning!

- Stick a lump of modeling clay to the middle of a metal baking sheet. Holding the clay, rub the sheet around on a plastic carrier bag.
- Then hold a metal lid from a jar close to the corner of the tray and watch as a spark of static electricity jumps between the lid and the metal sheet!

Noise and light

A flash of lightning is incredibly hot and, as it travels, the air around it suddenly expands in the heat, causing a loud bang of thunder. We hear the thunder after the lightning because sound travels more slowly through the air than light does. The roar of a really loud thunderclap can make the ground shake.

Lightning strikes a building in Shanghai, China.

Lightning conductors

Before 1752, dozens of church spires and towers were destroyed by lightning strikes every year. Then the lightning conductor was invented. This is a metal strip or rod that runs from the high point of a building down to the ground and conducts, or carries, the electricity from the lightning safely to the ground.

It's Amazing!

American forest ranger Roy Sullivan got the nickname the "Human Lightning Rod" because he holds the world record for being struck by lightning more times than anyone else in the world! Between 1942 and his death in 1983, Sullivan was struck by lightning seven times.

Storm clouds

One cumulonimbus cloud can hold as much water as 2,000 Olympic-sized swimming pools. When this water suddenly falls as rain over a short period of time, it can cause rivers to overflow, flooding streets and houses.

These houses in Hungary were flooded after a sudden storm caused rivers to burst their banks.

Floods

When a flood happens, buildings and roads can be washed away, people can drown, clean water supplies can be contaminated, and crops can be ruined. Across the world, floods are the most frequent weather-related disaster.

Flooding caused by monsoon rains in India in 2000

Regular floods

In India and parts of Southeast Asia, annual monsoon rains fall in a wet season that regularly brings floods. The powerful rains often fill streets, and even entire cities, with water.

River floods

The most common, and usually the worst, floods happen when a river overflows its banks. When a lot of rain falls in a short time, the soil becomes saturated and the rain flows off it into rivers instead of draining into the ground. A large flood can swell a river to ten times its normal depth.

Summer meltwater off this glacier (see pages 172–173) in Norway swells local streams and can cause flooding.

Snowmelts

In spring, the snow and ice that has covered the mountains during winter starts to thaw and turn into water. When this 'meltwater' flows down into the river valleys, it sometimes creates floods by causing the rivers to burst their banks.

The result of a flash flood in Great Britain

Sea floods

A sea flood is one that covers low-lying coastal land, and it can be caused by heavy storms. When strong winds blow on the sea, they can make the water swell up. When the big waves wash into the shore, they go much farther inland than usual. If a storm surge happens at high tide—when sea water has risen to its highest point—the flooding can be even more dangerous.

Flash floods

A flash flood is one that appears and travels quickly, with little warning that it is coming. Flash floods usually happen when a heavy storm drops a lot of rain in a short time and over a fairly small area. Flash floods turn gentle rivers into raging torrents, and the fast-moving water can knock over almost anything in its path.

It's Amazing!

Only 5 inches of rushing water is deep enough to knock down and drown a person. About 2 feet of water on a road can make a car or even a bus float!

Top Facts

- 95 percent of people killed in flash floods try to outrun flood water rather than climb to high ground.

- Rainwater cannot soak into ground covered in concrete, so in cities there are storm drains to carry away water that would cause flooding.

Heavy rains have created this torrent of water in the Italian city of Genoa.

Drought

A drought happens when an area has an unusually long period without any rainfall. All living things need water, and a drought can kill crops and livestock, bringing famine and starvation and altering the quality of the soil for a long time.

Women carry water from a well during a drought in India.

Why does it stop raining?

Many parts of the world experience regular dry seasons that usually end when the rain comes. If no rain falls, there is a drought. Droughts happen in areas that usually get enough rain to support life. Some places have short droughts, when high-pressure weather systems linger for several weeks, preventing low-pressure weather systems that bring rain from moving in. In some areas, high-pressure systems stay, and the drought can last for several years.

Elephants visit a shrinking water hole in Kenya.

Drought effects

During a drought, the soil loses the nutrients that plants need to grow. Plants die and ponds and rivers dry up. Without water or plants, plant-eating animals, such as elephants and zebras, may starve. The meat eaters who feed on these plant eaters feel the affects later when the number of animals they can hunt declines.

American Dust Bowl

The Dust Bowl drought of the 1930s was one of the worst weather disasters in the history of the United States. It caused soil in the already over-farmed Great Plains region of North America to become so dry that it turned to dust. Winds blew clouds of dust so thick that they blocked out the sun for days at a time.

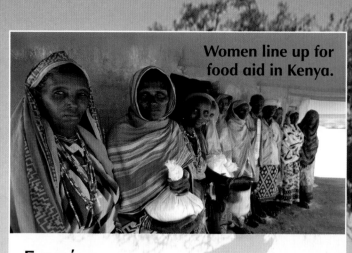
Women line up for food aid in Kenya.

Famine

A famine happens when a large number of people do not have enough to eat. In poor countries, during a drought, millions of people may rely on food aid brought in from abroad.

Where do droughts happen?

Droughts occur most often in regions of the world with hot, dry climates, such as parts of Africa, Australia, and the United States. Today, droughts are happening more often, partly because of human activity. People use more water than ever, making the problem of water shortages worse.

It's Amazing!

Throughout history, drought has killed more people and ruined more crops than any other type of natural disaster.

Water levels in this reservoir in Great Britain sank to low levels during a drought in 2006.

Drought restrictions

Countries with temperate climates, such as France and Great Britain, may experience mild droughts during hot summers. If water levels in reservoirs drop, governments restrict the amount of water people use. Fountains are switched off, people have to water their plants with waste water, and factories and power plants have to conserve water.

Heat wave

A heat wave occurs when a region experiences a period of unusually high temperatures. A heat wave may last just a day, but can go on for several weeks. The extreme heat and often high humidity can be uncomfortable—and even deadly.

Why heat waves happen

Heat waves happen in the summer when the air is hot and dry and a high-pressure weather system lingers for a long time. When the heat combines with high humidity, the temperature keeps on rising. The moisture in the air acts like a blanket and traps the heat, making it feel even warmer.

Australia heat wave

From December 1938 to February 1939, a heat wave in southern Australia caused 438 deaths and seriously affected many thousands of people. The highest recorded temperature was in the state of Victoria, and reached 118 degrees Farenheit.

Heat and humidity

Humidity is the amount of water vapor in the air. It is usually recorded as a percentage of the maximum amount of water vapor that the air can contain. High levels of humidity can worsen the effects of a heat wave. The combination of heat and moisture in the air makes people feel much warmer than the actual air temperature.

—— Temperatures above this line may cause heatstroke.

Air temperature (°F)	Relative humidity (%)																				
	0	5	10	15	20	25	30	35	40	45	50	55	60	65	70	75	80	85	90	95	100
140	125																				
135	120	128																			
130	117	122	131																		
125	111	116	123	131	141																
120	107	111	116	123	130	139	148														
115	103	101	111	115	120	127	135	143	151												
110	99	102	105	108	112	117	123	130	137	143	150										
105	95	97	100	102	105	109	113	118	123	129	135	142	149								
100	91	93	95	97	99	101	104	107	110	115	120	126	132	138	144						
95	87	88	90	91	93	94	96	98	101	104	107	110	114	119	124	130	136				
90	83	84	85	86	87	88	90	91	93	95	96	98	100	102	106	109	113	117	122		
85	78	79	80	81	82	83	84	85	86	87	88	89	90	91	93	95	97	99	102	105	108
80	73	74	75	76	77	77	78	79	79	80	81	81	82	83	85	86	86	87	88	89	91
75	69	69	70	71	72	72	73	73	74	74	75	75	76	76	77	77	78	78	79	79	80
70	64	64	65	65	66	66	67	67	68	68	69	69	70	70	70	70	71	71	71	71	72

The figures in this chart show how hot it feels when the air temperature and the humidity are combined.

Why heat waves kill

For humans, the ideal internal body temperature is 98.6 degrees Farenheit. If it rises above 104 degrees Farenheit, people can get heatstroke, which causes headaches, dizziness, and cramps—and even death. When people sweat to cool down, they lose moisture, and if this moisture is not replaced, they can become dehydrated. Water is vital to the body's health and being severely dehydrated can also be fatal.

A hot day in Berlin, Germany, during a heat wave in 2006

°Farenheit

110
100
90
80

It's Amazing!

For six weeks in the summer of 2006, most of the United States sweltered in a heat wave. In Los Angeles, California, the temperature reached a record high of 120 degrees Farenheit!

City heat waves

The buildings and roads in a city can make heatwaves hotter there than in the country. Buildings and roads absorb the sun's rays rather than reflect them, increasing daytime temperatures. This heat is released at night, a time when people should be cooling down. The lack of open space and heat from machines and vehicles makes the problem even worse in cities.

Advice during a heat wave

- Avoid going outside between 11:00 a.m. and 3:00 p.m.
- Take cool showers or baths several times a day.
- Eat cold food, salads, and juicy fruits.
- Drink a lot of water, and take water with you if you go out.
- Check on elderly neighbors.

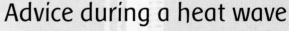

Wildfires

A wildfire is a fire that spreads quickly and uncontrollably through an area of forest, bush, or scrubland. Wildfires can be huge and last for many days, causing widespread damage to natural landscapes, property, and people.

This wildfire in Tasmania in 1967 had a fire danger index rating of 100.

The fire danger index

The factors that increase the likelihood of a wildfire breaking out include drought and low humidity. Meteorologists compile a fire danger index that starts at zero for the lowest risk of a fire breaking out and goes up to 100 for the highest risk.

Hot, dry seasons

Large wildfires happen during hot, dry seasons or times of drought. When no rain falls, the plants dry out. This means they are more likely to catch fire. After a wildfire has started, winds spread the flames or toss sparks or embers from a main fire on to new areas to start secondary blazes.

A wildfire rages on the outskirts of Townsville, Australia

The wooden buildings built in many countries burn easily in a wildfire.

Wildfire damage

Wildfires destroy large areas of forest, which supply the planet with oxygen and take hundreds of years to regrow. Forests are also home to many animals that may die or lose their homes in wildfires. Because wildfires spread quickly, they sometimes reach towns and destroy homes and even kill people.

How wildfires start

Some wildfires start when a bolt of lightning hits dry vegetation. Other wildfires are started by accident—because people are careless with campfires or cigarettes. A few fires may be started on purpose by criminals called arsonists.

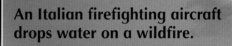

An Italian firefighting aircraft drops water on a wildfire.

Top Facts

- **Winds regularly spread wildfires at up to 15 miles per hour.**
- **Today, people start about 90 percent of wildfires; lightning only starts the other 10 percent.**
- **Fires happen regularly in forests and wild land, which cover one third of the planet's land surface.**

Stop the fires?

Although wildfires are destructive, they can help a forest. When rain washes ash from burned plants into the ground, it makes the soil more fertile. Fire also reduces the number of trees in a forest, allowing new plants to grow. Wildfires near towns must be put out, but some believe that other fires should be left to burn themselves out.

Blizzards

A blizzard is a severe winter storm that brings a great deal of snow or ice. To be a blizzard, a storm must have winds that blow at speeds greater than 30 miles per hour, rating seven or more on the Beaufort Wind Scale (see page 29). It must also reduce visibility to 380 yards or less for at least three hours.

Blizzard of 1888

In 1888, a blizzard covered large parts of the United States. In Connecticut and Massachusetts, more than 3 feet of snow fell and winds piled up in 50-foot-deep snowdrifts. Houses and trains were buried. In all, more than 400 people died.

This building in New York State collapsed after snow piled up on its roof in 1999.

Snow damage

Strong blizzard winds blow snow into huge piles of snow called snowdrifts. When snow builds up on buildings, its weight can make them collapse. Blizzards and freezing temperatures can cause power cuts and freeze water pipes, which may crack and burst.

How blizzards form

Blizzards happen when a mass of cold air collides with a mass of warm air. The warm air rises quickly, and the cold air cuts beneath it. This causes a cloud to form. When the air temperature between the cloud and the ground is cold, snow falls from the cloud. Strong winds blow the snow around, causing a blizzard. Warm air flowing up a mountainside can also form clouds that bring blizzards.

A cross-country skier struggles through a blizzard in Minnesota.

Where blizzards happen

Blizzards form only in areas outside the tropics. Masses of warm, moist air flow out of the tropics and meet cold air that is moving away from the North and South poles. The warm and cold air interact, creating the high winds and heavy snowfall that are typical of blizzards. The most destructive blizzards happen in places that are really cold in winter, such as the north of the United States and much of Canada.

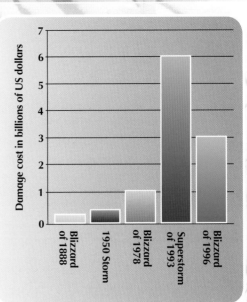

It's Amazing!

In mountain regions, blizzard winds can reach speeds of 100 miles per hour. They can tear off roofs, causing severe damage to property.

Blizzard damage

Blizzards can cause huge amounts of damage in terms of property and loss of life. The North American blizzard of 1888, for example, sank 200 ships and killed 400 people. In more recent years, the winter storms in the United States in 1993 caused more than 6 billion dollars of damage.

Transport chaos

Blizzards make transport and travel almost impossible because drivers cannot see where they are going. The extremely low temperatures can harm anyone caught or stranded outside in a blizzard. People may get frostbite (see page 25). Large snowdrifts can block roads, making them impassable, and thick ice can bring down power lines and damage tracks on railroad networks.

Strong winds blow from Hurricane Katrina in 2005.

Strong winds

A spiraling wind becomes a hurricane when it reaches speeds of 75 miles per hour. Some hurricanes spin at 210 miles per hour, which is as fast as a high-speed train!

Hurricanes

Hurricanes are powerful and destructive storms with violent, spinning winds. These tropical storms form over warm seas, but weaken as they move over land. Some big hurricanes travel a long way inland, leaving a path of destruction.

How hurricanes happen

Hurricanes form in the warm, moist air over hot ocean waters. The warm air rises into the atmosphere and, as it does so, more damp air fills the space left behind. This air gets warmer and starts to rise as well. Soon, strong winds are blowing up around the low-pressure center of the hurricane.

Hurricane's eye

The center of a hurricane is called its eye, and this may be 18 to 36 miles wide. Within the eye the winds do not blow, and it is eerily calm. Hurricanes move along as they spin. When a hurricane passes directly overhead, people experience high winds followed by a calm spell, when the eye is directly above them, followed by high winds once again.

Air spirals around the eye and cools.

Eye

Warm, moist air rises.

Hurricane winds and rain

Why hurricanes spin

As the warm air rises, it creates an area of low pressure. Cool air continues to rush into this low-pressure area, but it is deflected by the Coriolis Effect (see page 30). This deflection is caused by the moving air being dragged by the planet as it rotates. In the northern hemisphere, the air is deflected to the right. This creates a spiral, like water going down a drain, with the hurricane spinning counterclockwise. In the southern hemisphere, the winds are deflected to the left, which means that hurricanes here spin clockwise.

(see page 30)

Satellite image of Hurricane Elena from 1985, showing the bands of cloud spiraling counterclockwise around the eye

It's Amazing!
Some hurricanes are a few hundred miles wide, but the largest can be as big as 600 miles across!

Damage left by Hurricane Katrina after it struck New Orleans in 2005

Hurricane damage

As well as damaging winds, hurricanes and typhoons bring torrential rain that can cause floods, landslides, and giant waves. They blow down buildings, rip out trees, and toss cars and ships around like toys. Such storms have killed thousands of people. Scientists track the storms and try to warn people before they strike.

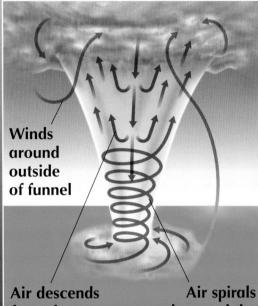

Winds around outside of funnel

Air descends from the cloud.

Air spirals upward around the tornado's funnel.

Inside a tornado

The winds in a tornado spiral around the narrow eye and rise up the funnel. These strong rising currents of air can suck up cars, trees, and houses and also pull some air down from the cloud above the tornado.

Tornadoes

Tornadoes are tall, thin funnels of spiraling winds that stretch down from tall cumulonimbus clouds and touch the ground. Tornadoes are often called twisters. They are much smaller and faster than hurricanes and do not last as long, but they, too, can cause terrible destruction.

It's Amazing!

There have been tornadoes with wind speeds of 300 miles per hour and some that move across land at up to 40 miles per hour.

How tornadoes form and die

Tornadoes form over land. They begin when an updraft—a current of warm, moist air rising through a thunderstorm—meets a mass of cold, dry air. The rising warm air causes the cold air to be dragged down. The updraft rises higher and starts to rotate. Tornadoes die out over colder ground or when the cumulonimbus clouds above them break up.

A tornado touches the ground in a cornfield in Kansas in 2001.

This waterspout, photographed in 1945, had a base that was nearly 500 feet wide.

Waterspouts

Like tornadoes, waterspouts are rapidly rotating columns of air, but they extend from a cumulonimbus cloud down to an area of water, such as a lake, river, or sea. Waterspouts range in size from just 30 feet to 5,000 feet high, sucking up water as they spin. They only last for a short time, but look dramatic and can damage ships at sea.

Where tornadoes happen

Tornadoes can happen anywhere in the world with the right combination of warm, damp winds and cold, dry winds. A large area of the central United States, including Kansas, Arkansas, and Oklahoma, is known as Tornado Alley. Many tornadoes happen here because cool, dry air from Canada crashes into warm, humid air from the Gulf of Mexico.

Top Facts

- Tornadoes happen in places as far apart as Australia, Italy, Bangladesh, and Great Britain.

- The path of destruction left in the wake of a tornado can be 1¼ miles wide and 45 miles long!

Raining toads!

Tornadoes and waterspouts often suck up unusual objects, such as frogs, toads, and fish. These can then fall from the sky somewhere else. In Mexico in June 1997, a tornado carried a group of live toads from a pool of water and dropped them all over a nearby town!

Sandstorms

Sandstorms occur when strong winds blow large amounts of sand or dust around in the air. They form huge clouds that block out the sunlight. The sand and dust make it difficult for people to breathe, stop aircraft flying, close businesses and schools, injure animals, and damage crops.

How sandstorms happen

Sandstorms form over dry land when air warmed by heat from the ground rises rapidly. Cooler air takes the place of the hot air. As it cools, the hot air sinks again, creating a circular current called a convection current. These air currents whip dust and sand into the air. The wind tosses them around violently and carries them long distances.

Top Facts

- Sand and dust particles travel vast distances on a rising air current, reaching high above the ground. They blow down later on a sinking current.

- Sandstorms and dust storms reduce visibility and cause traffic accidents.

- Dust storms can travel at speeds of up to 75 miles per hour.

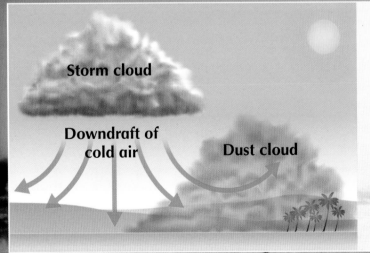

Storm cloud

Downdraft of cold air

Dust cloud

What is a "haboob"?

"Haboob" is the Arabic for "violent wind." A haboob is a type of sandstorm that happens in very dry regions, such as northern Africa, India, and, during the summer, Arizona. Haboobs form when cold air blows down from a thunderstorm. The downdraft lifts dust or sand into the air and tosses it about violently, forming a huge cloud.

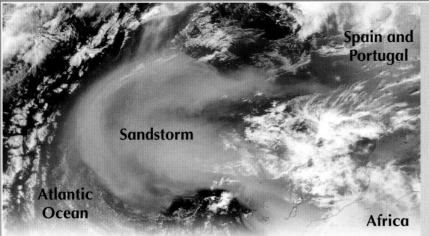

Spain and Portugal

Sandstorm

Atlantic Ocean

Africa

A sandstorm blows off the Sahara in 2000.

Sahara storms

In the Sahara in Africa, rising warm air can lift dust 5,000 yards above the desert and then out over the Atlantic. Few people live in the desert, so storms there cause little disruption. But the dust can blow across the ocean to the Caribbean, where it has damaged coral reefs and made it difficult for people to breathe.

Super sandstorms

Sandstorms are often vast, and some can move entire sand dunes. They can carry so much sand or dust that the leading edge of a storm can appear as a solid wall more than a mile high! Winds in the Gobi desert often create huge dust storms that drift over the Pacific Ocean. The storms usually die out above the water as there is no more dust to pick up.

It's Amazing!

Sandstorms on Mars are much bigger than on Earth because Mars is covered in dust. In 2001, an enormous sandstorm on Mars covered the entire surface of the planet.

Chinese women cover their mouths during a sandstorm in 2006.

Yellow dust

Every year during the dry spring season, high-speed surface winds carry huge clouds of sandy, yellow dust from the deserts of Mongolia and northern China across China and Korea. This dust causes eye and breathing problems and people often wear masks to protect their faces.

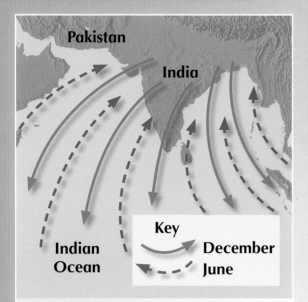

Pakistan

India

Indian Ocean

Key

December

June

Indian monsoon

The Indian monsoon brings the highest rainfall of any of the monsoon winds. It will usually start in the middle of June when the monsoon winds switch to blowing inland off the Indian Ocean. By September, the rains have finished and the winds start to reverse their direction.

Monsoon winds

A monsoon is a seasonal wind that changes its direction every six months. In the winter, the monsoon wind will blow from the land to the sea, and in summer it will blow from the sea to the land, bringing wet air and heavy rains.

What causes monsoons?

Monsoon winds are created by the temperature difference between large land masses and the ocean. Cool, moist air from the ocean blows in to fill the gap left by warm air rising over the land in summer, bringing wind and heavy rain. As the land cools, the winds change direction and blow from land to sea, bringing dry weather.

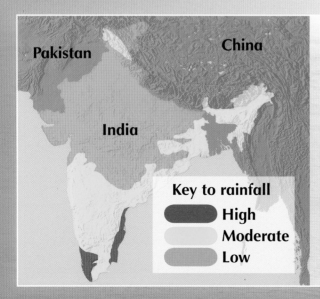

Pakistan

China

India

Key to rainfall

High

Moderate

Low

The moving monsoon

Because the summer monsoon winds blow off the Indian Ocean, the monsoon rains start in the south of India. These regions will receive the most rain. The average annual rainfall for India is 35 inches, but some regions that experience heavy monsoon rains have an average annual rainfall of 36 feet.

Three seasons

In India and other parts of southern Asia, there are three distinct seasons. There is a cool, dry winter season that runs from October to March. This is followed in April and May by the region's hottest and driest weather. Temperatures in this season can be almost unbearable. When the monsoon arrives in June, there are often scenes of rejoicing on the streets!

A footbridge in Nepal is ruined by floods caused by the monsoon of 1987.

Monsoon damage

The monsoon rains are too heavy to soak into the dry soil, causing rivers to overflow. The floods damage homes, roads and railroads, and affect animals and people. The rains also flood dry fields, allowing farmers to plant rice and other crops.

A woman paddles through flooding caused by the Indian monsoon of 2003.

It's Amazing!

During the monsoon season, India is the wettest place in the world. The monsoon rains account for 80 percent of the country's total rainfall.

Top Facts

- The temperature difference between the land and sea during the monsoon can be as much as 36°F.

- The rains brought by the monsoon are vital to India's farming industry and the country's economy. After a strong monsoon in 2004, the country's economy grew by 8.5 percent.

El Niño

El Niño is a big warm ocean current that develops every two to seven years in the Pacific Ocean. It causes extreme weather around the world. An El Niño event lasts about 12 to 18 months.

On the move

A patch of water as warm as a bath and the size of Europe sits in the Pacific off Australia. It is kept in place by strong trade winds blowing west. In El Niño years, the winds slacken, and the warm water gradually flows across the ocean toward Peru and California.

It's Amazing!

The worst El Niño of recent times lasted from December 1982 to January 1983. Australia had terrible droughts, and Peru had its heaviest ever rainfall, turning deserts to wetlands.

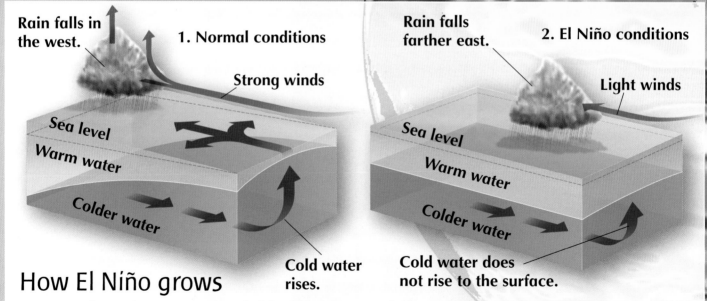

Rain falls in the west.   **1. Normal conditions**

Strong winds

Sea level

Warm water

Colder water

Cold water rises.

Rain falls farther east.   **2. El Niño conditions**

Light winds

Sea level

Warm water

Colder water

Cold water does not rise to the surface.

How El Niño grows

In normal conditions (1), winds blowing west push the surface water, causing the sea level to be higher in the western Pacific than the eastern. This causes colder water to rise to the surface in the eastern Pacific, making the water much colder than in the western Pacific. During El Niño (2), the winds weaken and warm water flows to the eastern Pacific, bringing more humid air and heavy rain with it.

Weather patterns

The warm, humid air mass above the warm waters of the western Pacific normally creates tropical storms that blow across Indonesia and northern Australia. In El Niño years, the flow of warm water to the eastern Pacific causes storms to hit the eastern Pacific coast instead, bringing wetter weather.

North America

Pacific Ocean

South America

This satellite image shows the temperature of the Pacific in different colors, with purple being coldest and white the hottest.

Key

Hotter

Colder

What is La Niña?

La Niña, meaning "the girl," often follows El Niño and is its opposite. Trade winds strengthen and warm water piles up in the western Pacific, bringing stormy weather to eastern Asia and dry, cold weather to western North and South America.

North America

Pacific Ocean

South America

During La Niña, the eastern Pacific has a larger area of cool water.

Effects of El Niño

While El Niño causes heavy rains and flooding on the eastern side of the Pacific, it has the opposite effect on the western side. Here, little rain falls, causing droughts, heat waves, and wildfires.

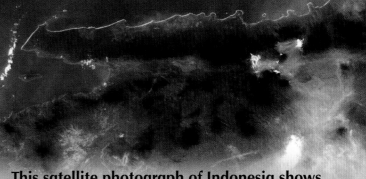

This satellite photograph of Indonesia shows smoke from wildfires caused during El Niño.

WEATHER DISASTERS

It is only when the weather is extreme that we really take notice of it. Across the world, dangerous and unusual weather has caused suffering to millions of people. Avalanches and mud slides, heat waves and hurricanes, droughts and floods are just some of these devastating weather events. In this chapter, we look in detail at some of the worst weather disasters in recent times, and see what effect they had on the people who witnessed them.

Hurricane Katrina, New Orleans

When Hurricane Katrina struck parts of Louisiana, Mississippi, and Alabama on August 29, 2005, it became the deadliest hurricane to hit the United States for more than 75 years. The winds and floods brought by Hurricane Katrina killed about 1,850 people.

Cars and trucks jam the freeway during the evacuation of New Orleans.

Hurricane warning

Hurricane Katrina started to form on August 23 during the 2005 Atlantic hurricane season. It gradually gained strength, and on August 28 a hurricane warning was declared for Louisiana, Mississippi, and Alabama. People were told to evacuate, or leave, their homes in New Orleans and along the Gulf Coast. Katrina hit the Louisiana coast on August 29, and traveled inland, causing damage up to 150 miles from the sea.

Where it happened

Hurricane Katrina built up over the Caribbean Sea, blew inland and hit Florida briefly, then returned to the sea. There, it gained strength before blowing inland from the Gulf of Mexico and hitting New Orleans and the Gulf Coast. It finally died out over Mississippi.

Broken levees

New Orleans suffered severe flooding. Both the Mississippi River, which runs through the center of the city, and a lake to its north are at higher levels than the city itself. To prevent floods, high banks of earth called levees surround New Orleans. Unfortunately, Hurricane Katrina caused floods to break through parts of the levees. When the defenses broke, about 80 percent of the city filled with water.

A woman takes refuge in the Superdome.

It's Amazing!

In the year after Katrina, the U.S. Salvation Army served more than 5.7 million hot meals and 8.3 million sandwiches to people affected by the disaster.

In the stadium

The people of New Orleans were warned to evacuate, but many either chose not to or could not leave. About 26,000 people sheltered in the Superdome stadium—the city's official shelter. They had little food or water, and conditions there were very uncomfortable.

A house and a car destroyed by the hurricane.

Terrible destruction

Winds of more than 125 miles per hour peeled roofs off buildings, blasted out windows and blew down power lines. The floodwater blocked roads and vehicles were hurled around the streets. In total, about 78,000 homes were destroyed in New Orleans alone.

Top Facts

- Following the order to evacuate, about 500,000 people fled New Orleans. A year later, only about 200,000 people had returned to the city.

- About 5,000 children were separated from their families in the disaster.

Oklahoma tornadoes

Tornadoes occur in Oklahoma and Kansas every year, but in May 1999, there was a tornado disaster. A number of tornadoes hit the area at once, killing 47 people, destroying 2,000 homes and causing terrible damage.

Tornado swarms

A swarm is when a lot of tornadoes happen at once. Tornado swarms can be particularly dangerous. In May 1999, 74 tornadoes touched down across Oklahoma and Kansas in less than 21 hours. Some of the tornadoes in Oklahoma measured about 1 mile wide, with winds of more than 175 miles per hour. The biggest tornado hit the outskirts of Oklahoma City.

Top Facts

- Many people survived the Oklahoma tornadoes because they took shelter in a basement or a storm cellar.

- A tornado can move as fast as a speeding car and can change direction extremely quickly.

- Rescue workers use specially trained dogs to sniff out victims buried below collapsed buildings.

Where it happened

The wide flat area between the Rocky Mountains and the Mississippi River is known as "Tornado Alley." Cold, dry air moving in from Canada clashes with warm, moist air from the Gulf of Mexico there. This creates huge storm clouds that can lead to tornadoes.

Tornado Alley

Kansas

Oklahoma

• Oklahoma City

Gulf of Mexico

It's Amazing!

Most tornadoes are small and last from only a few seconds up to 30 minutes. But the tornado that struck Oklahoma City touched the ground for 90 minutes and covered about 40 miles!

Early warning

Although the Oklahoma tornadoes were terrible, many people were saved thanks to early-warning systems. Weather forecasters used information from radars and helicopter crews to follow the path of the tornadoes. They gave warnings on radio and television to people in Oklahoma and nearby areas to evacuate. Police officers even walked the streets warning residents, so everyone knew there was a danger and had time to leave their homes before the tornadoes passed through.

This whole street in Oklahoma City was destroyed by the tornadoes.

A tornado forms in southwest Oklahoma. Most of the damage happens where the funnel hits the ground.

Airborne destruction

Tornadoes in this region usually speed across the countryside. What made the May 1999 tornado so bad was that it charged through cities. Oklahoma City was said to look like a bomb site. The spiraling winds acted like giant vacuum cleaners, sucking up mobile homes, trees, and vehicles and tossing them in the air.

Reduced to rubble

When people inspected the scene after the tornadoes had passed through, they saw streets reduced to rubble. The air was full of dust from all the homes and furniture that had been broken up. Most people were just glad to be alive despite losing their homes.

Home owners look for belongings in the debris of their ruined house.

Galtür avalanche

An avalanche happens when snow and ice suddenly slip down a mountain side. Small avalanches are hardly noticed in high mountains, but larger avalanches can bury whole towns, knocking down trees and buildings in their path. In February 1999, there was an avalanche disaster in the village of Galtür in Austria.

Where it happened

Galtür is a village in the Paznaun Valley in Austria. The valley has high snowy slopes and is a popular ski resort. In January and February 1999, about 9 feet of snow fell on the village—the most for 50 years.

Moving slab

At 4:00 p.m. on Tuesday February 23, the snow and ice cover finally became too heavy to stick to the mountain slope. It broke off and slid down the mountain side at 180 miles per hour, carrying trees and boulders with it. By the time it hit the bottom of the valley, this moving slab of snow, ice and debris was about 110 yards high and 550 yards wide. It completely engulfed the village of Galtür.

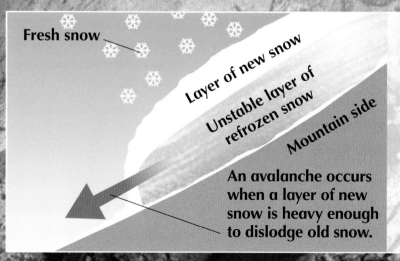

Fresh snow

Layer of new snow

Unstable layer of refrozen snow

Mountain side

An avalanche occurs when a layer of new snow is heavy enough to dislodge old snow.

Unstable layers

Avalanches occur when changing temperatures create a layer of unstable snow. This is snow that has melted, refrozen, and become slippery. The unstable layer is more likely to slip down a slope after heavy snow.

Top Facts

- Nearly 80 percent of all avalanche deaths happen in the United States, Austria, France, and Switzerland, where there are many ski resorts.

- Many avalanches are triggered accidentally by people, for example, when using snowmobiles. Sometimes, they are started on purpose high in mountains to stop snow from piling up and becoming dangerous.

Rescue!

At Galtür, the snow froze hard and rescuers had to poke long metal probes into it to locate survivors. There was also a rescue dog in the village that helped to sniff out people buried under the snow.

Rescuers attempt to locate survivors in the snowdrifts.

After the avalanche

The avalanche pushed cars out of the way like toys, and sliced off the top of some houses. There were 60 people trapped under the snow, and of them, 31 died from being crushed by falling buildings, hypothermia, or suffocation. While rescue teams tried to find the survivors, other helpers evacuated those who had lost their homes. This was made more difficult because heavy snow prevented helicopters from flying in and other, smaller avalanches had blocked many roads.

Airborne photo of ruined buildings in Galtür, just after the avalanche

It's Amazing!

Dogs can smell human survivors buried under 13 feet or more of snow. They can smell the bacteria on our skin 1,000 times better than we can!

Australian bush fires

On Monday January 10, 2005, bush fires began to spread throughout the Eyre Peninsula in South Australia. Emergency services worked to control the fires, but weather conditions helped to spread the blaze and, by the end of the day on January 11, the flames had caused devastation across a massive area.

Hot and dry

The fires began at the time of the worst drought on record for South Australia. There had been so little rainfall that all the forest and grassland plants were extremely dry. The weather was also very hot, with temperatures exceeding 104 degrees Fahrenheit.

Top Facts

- The forest included a large number of eucalyptus trees—with oily leaves that burn easily.

- Southeastern Australia is more likely to have bush fires than anywhere else in the world.

- Many animals were killed, including about 250,000 sheep and 500 cattle.

It's Amazing!

More than 300 firefighters and 80 fire trucks were involved in battling the devastating blaze in the Eyre Peninsula.

Where it happened

Eyre Peninsula is a long headland in South Australia. Driven by strong winds, the fires raced down the peninsula toward the sea until the entire peninsula was cut off. Some people escaped by swimming out into the sea, where they were rescued by helicopter.

AUSTRALIA

• Adelaide

Eyre Peninsula

Wind-fanned flames

Most of the blazes in the Eyre Peninsula were started by lightning strikes. The fires were spread by high winds with speeds of up to 45 miles per hour. The winds not only fed existing flames, but also blew burning embers to other areas and created new, "spot" fires. The winds continued to blow and spread the spot fires, which grew and combined with the main fires.

Flames rage out of control on the Eyre Peninsula on January 11.

A helicopter drops water on areas of the fire that the fire crews cannot reach.

This satellite photograph of the Eyre Peninsula was taken on January 11.

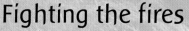

Fires

Smoke

Seen from above

The smoke from the fires spread out over a huge distance. About 200,000 acres of land were damaged and 73 houses were destroyed, along with farm buildings, cars, and buses. Nine people were killed in the fires, and 110 people were injured. Eight out of the nine who died were trying to outrun the flames in their cars.

Fighting the fires

By January 11, firefighters seemed to have the fire under control. But strong winds then spread the fire at a rate the firefighters could not stop. On Wednesday, January 12, using helicopters to dump water from above, they stopped the blaze from spreading. It finally went out completely a few days later.

Ethiopian drought

Ethiopia and Somalia are neighboring countries that frequently have droughts, many of which have caused widespread famine. In 1984, there was a drought in which almost one million people died. In 2004, both countries were affected by drought again and millions of people needed food aid.

Reasons for the drought

Lowland regions of Ethiopia and Somalia have two rainy seasons a year and two very hot, dry seasons. Rainfall is low and temperatures are high all year. There is only about 20 inches of rain a year, and this is very unreliable so droughts often occur. In 2004, the rainy seasons were late and brought very little rain, resulting in the harvests failing.

Top Facts

- Some droughts can last for five, or even ten years.
- About 85 percent of the 67 million people in Ethiopia are farmers.
- When harvests fail, African farmers sell their animals to pay for food but, once these are sold, they have nothing.

It's Amazing!

In times of drought, shepherds, who can usually find water for their flocks by digging 6½ feet into dry riverbeds, have to dig down as deep as 26 feet!

Where it happened

Ethiopia and Somalia are large countries in the Horn of Africa, a very dry area in northeastern Africa on the edge of the Sahara. In the past, severe droughts occurred there every ten years or so. In recent times, they have happened at least every three years.

SUDAN
ERITREA
YEMEN
ETHIOPIA
SOMALIA
Horn of Africa
KENYA
Indian Ocean

Foreign aid

The Ethiopian government stores some emergency food, but there was not enough in 2004, so aid was flown in from around the world. Planes brought food, medicine, blankets, and clothes, as well as tools and seeds for farmers. Aid organizations also sent medical workers to treat sick people.

An Ethiopian man carries a bag of wheat donated by the United States.

This Ethiopian family have left their village and are walking to find food aid.

Famine

When it did not rain in 2004, the crops died, and without plants to eat, the cattle and goats died, too. People started to suffer from malnutrition—an illness caused by lack of food—and they became very weak or died. Clean water supplies dried up, and some people became dehydrated or caught diseases caused by drinking dirty water.

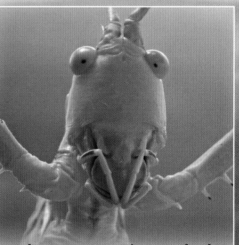

A locust can eat its own body weight in food each day.

Pest swarms

Swarms of locusts fly across Africa, eating everything green in their path. When this happens, a drought is made much worse.

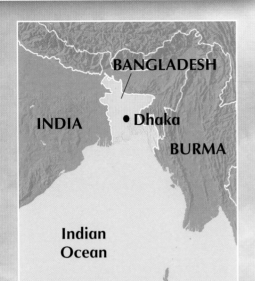

INDIA

BANGLADESH

• Dhaka

BURMA

Indian
Ocean

Where it happened

Bangladesh is on a delta, where three rivers—the Ganges, the Brahmaputra, and the Meghna—flow into the ocean. In most years, people cope with the floods by traveling in boats and living in houses built on stilts. But in 2004, the floods were too deep.

Bangladesh flood

Bangladesh is a low-lying country in Asia. Each year, during the monsoon seasons, floods affect one third of the country. In 2004, there was flooding over two thirds of the country, affecting 30 million people.

Double flooding

The monsoon rains in July 2004 caused many rivers in the north to burst their banks. The floods started to drop at the end of August, but in the second week of September, a mass of warm, humid air blew in from the Indian Ocean. This caused three times the normal rainfall for the time of year, and increased the floodwaters.

It's Amazing!

The United Nations estimates that, by 2025, half the world's people will be living in areas at risk from floods, storms, and other extreme weather disasters.

A family who have lost their home are living in a temporary shelter.

Survivors

Survivors of the floods were forced to flee their villages. Thousands streamed into refugee centers—especially in the capital city of Dhaka. The Bangladeshi government and aid agencies provided food and medical care, temporary shelters, and help repairing damaged homes.

Sick people are treated in hospital in Dhaka.

Dirty water

Human waste became mixed with the water. Tens of thousands of people caught diseases, such as dysentery, after drinking the dirty water. Many were treated in hospital, but there was not enough medicine to go around.

Top Facts

- **During the monsoons, Bangladesh has heavy rainfall, which falls in rivers that are already full from snow melting in the Himalayas. This makes the rivers burst their banks.**

- **Poor people often live in high-risk areas, such as floodplains because land there is cheaper and may be all that is available.**

Aftermath

At least 800 people died in the 2004 floods— some by drowning and disease, others by electrocution from fallen power lines or bites from poisonous snakes in the water. For survivors, there were food shortages because food was lost or rotted in the damp conditions. There was little clean water to drink. Thousands of wells, toilets, roads, bridges, railroad tracks, and ditches were destroyed or swept away. Many farms and clothing factories were ruined.

This boy has to travel by boat to visit his flooded home.

Philippines mud slide

On February 17, 2006, after days of rain, a hillside collapsed and buried the isolated village of Guinsaugon on the island of Leyte in the southern Philippines. Villagers had been evacuated from the area, but most had returned when disaster struck.

Background to a tragedy

The Philippines usually have a rainy season between June and December. In 2006, the storms came late and were very heavy. Over 6½ feet of rain fell in ten days—about four times the maximum of any previous month. The rain waterlogged the soil on the side of a mountain overlooking Guinsaugon village, making it heavy and unstable. At 9:00 a.m. on February 17, the mud slide hit.

Top Facts

- About 740 million cubic feet of earth fell on the village.
- Cutting down trees may have made the mud slide worse, because trees absorb the rain and their roots hold the soil together.
- In 1991, 6,000 people were killed on Leyte in floods and mud slides.

It's Amazing!

When the mud slide settled, it had covered more than 10 million square feet of land and flattened about 300 homes.

CHINA

Pacific Ocean

VIETNAM

PHILIPPINES

South China Sea

• Leyte

Where it happened

Leyte is just one of 7,000 islands that make up the Philippines, although only 11 of these are inhabited. The village of Guinsaugon is very remote. It takes six hours to get there by road from the nearest airport in Leyte's capital, Tacloban. Annual rainfall in the Philippines is more than 3 feet almost everywhere, and temperatures remain high all year.

Devastation

The mud slide buried the whole village, including a school with 246 children and seven teachers inside, who had just started morning classes. When the mud settled it was up to 16 yards deep in some places, and only a few tin roofs and coconut trees were visible. In all, 1,800 people died in this terrible tragedy.

Soldiers dig in the mud, hoping to find life beneath the roof of a ruined house.

Filippino rescue workers arrive in the village to help search for survivors.

Mountain scar

The large scar left by the mud slide was clearly visible during the rescue mission. About 30 U.S. marines from ships that happened to be in the area were sent to help the villagers. Many other countries sent rescuers, as well as medical supplies and food.

Rescue efforts

Heavy rain hampered the rescue. At first, rescue workers had to use shovels to dig for survivors because the deep mud was too unstable to use mechanical diggers. Rescue teams brought sniffer dogs and heat sensors to help in the search for survivors, but only about 50 were pulled out alive.

A U.S. marine becomes stuck in the mud while helping in the rescue.

American blizzard

Blizzards are common in winter in parts of North America, but in some years, they are more severe than others. When heavy blizzards swept across large areas of the North in January 2005, about 20 people were killed, and transportation systems and daily lives were severely disrupted.

Snow conditions

In the blizzard of 2005, winds reached speeds of 50 miles per hour and these, combined with cold temperatures, created a light, fluffy snow. This kind of snow blows around easily, and caused near whiteout conditions with very low visibility. High winds blew snow into deep snowdrifts, trapping some people in their homes for up to 24 hours.

Top Facts

- The high winds in the 2005 blizzard caused extreme windchill, and there was concern that people caught outside might get frostbite or hypothermia.

- The weight of the snow brought down power lines and caused power outages in many areas.

- Salem and Plymouth in Massachusetts received a record 38 inches of snow.

This home in New England was completely covered in snow and ice.

Where it happened

The blizzard began over the north central parts of United States on January 20. It moved slowly east, reaching the Great Lakes region near the U.S.–Canadian border and parts of the Atlantic coast, such as New York City, on January 21 and 22. By January 23, the blizzard had also hit New England. The storm then traveled across the Atlantic Ocean and affected parts of Europe.

CANADA

Great Lakes

New England

New York City

USA

Atlantic Ocean

Transport troubles

Thousands of flights were canceled when planes were grounded because of the snow and high winds. In some areas, snow turned to ice, and it was so cold that salt put on roads to melt the ice did not work. Snow-removal crews found it hard to work in the strong winds, which blew piles of snow back onto the roads as soon as they had cleared them.

It's Amazing!

In New York, 2,500 workers, equipped with 1,800 pieces of equipment, such as snowplows, cleared the city's 6,000 miles of roads. The mayor said each inch of snow cost 1 million dollars to clear!

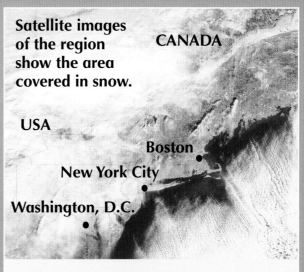

Satellite images of the region show the area covered in snow.

CANADA

USA

Boston

New York City

Washington, D.C.

Blizzard warnings

Weather forecasters in the United States studied satellite images like the one above, as well as temperature, wind direction, and speed, to decide where the blizzard was likely to hit. On January 24, they advised people to stay indoors because they predicted that temperatures would be extremely cold.

New York snowdrifts

New York was hit by up to 18 inches of snow. The city's mayor had warned people to be prepared for the blizzard, and many stocked up on food and supplies. Snowplows worked through the night to clear the roads, leaving piles of snow up to 10 feet deep on the sidewalks. The disruption would have been even worse if the blizzard had not hit over a weekend.

Traffic passes snow piled up in Times Square, New York City.

Chinese sandstorm

Sandstorms can cause extreme damage to crops, and can injure and even kill people and their animals. One of the world's hot spots for big sandstorms is northwest China. The sandstorm that hit Beijing in 2002 was the worst for ten years.

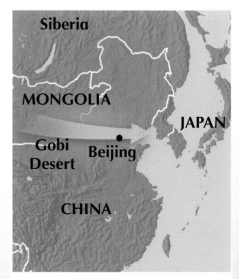

City transformed

The sandstorm struck on March 20, 2002. China's capital, Beijing, was swathed in ghostly light as the sky turned from gray to yellow to orange. About 45,000 tons of sand and dust were dumped on the city by high winds. Visibility was down to 220 yards in the city, and even less in the countryside to the northwest.

Where it happened

Very cold, high-pressure air sinking over Siberia in Russia pushed winds south and southeast over Mongolia and China. The winds picked up sand from the Gobi Desert and dumped some of it across northern China.

Traffic in Beijing struggles through the sandstorm.

Sand effects

About 100 million Chinese were affected by the sandstorm. Farmers lost their crops, flights were canceled and many people had breathing and eye problems. The storm spread from China to South Korea and Japan. The sand blew over the Pacific Ocean, where most dropped into the sea.

- **The Gobi Desert is expanding at a rate of 2.4 percent a year. Nearly three quarters of the land that was once grassland in northwest China is now desert.**

- **In some areas, the Chinese government offers free grain to farmers who convert their fields into shelterbelts.**

A man battles through the sandstorm on his way to work.

Desertification

The winds blowing from Russia pick up so much sand and dust because the Gobi Desert is getting bigger. This desertification is the gradual change from woodland, grassland, or scrubland to desert. It can happen naturally, but also because of over-farming. Grazing too many animals on the land kills the plants. Their roots no longer hold the soil together, and it dries and blows away.

Farmers plant trees in Xian in northern China.

Shelterbelts

Planting rows of trees called shelterbelts can prevent sand damage by sheltering settlements and crops from the wind. In previous sandstorms in China, farmers lost 85 percent of their crops, but after building shelterbelts, they lost only 5 percent of crops.

It's Amazing!

The 2002 sandstorm was so vast that it was visible as an enormous yellow stain on satellite images. It covered an area of approximately 5½ million square miles.

European heat wave

Tens of thousands of people died across Europe in the unusually hot summer of 2003. Scientists believe that the high temperatures may have been caused by global warming (see page 208).

Widespread effects

As many as 50,000 people died in the heat wave, including 20,000 in Italy and nearly 15,000 in France. The heat caused dehydration and overheating of the body, which is known as hyperthermia. Many who died were elderly people who did not have air conditioning in their homes. The heat affected the health of many more by causing heart attacks and accidents. People were also affected when crops failed in southern Europe, forests burned in Portugal, and glaciers melted in Switzerland, causing avalanches and floods.

Top Facts

- The 2003 heat wave was the biggest natural disaster to strike Europe.

- Many countries recorded their highest temperatures, and August 2003 was the hottest August in the Northern Hemisphere since records began.

- Some crops, such as grapes, actually did better in the heat.

People cool off in a fountain in Paris, France.

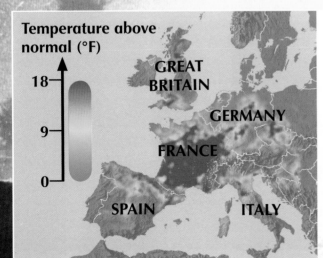

Temperature above normal (°F)

18 —
9 —
0 —

GREAT BRITAIN

GERMANY

FRANCE

SPAIN   ITALY

Where it happened

France, Germany, Poland, Switzerland, Austria, northern Spain and Portugal, northern Italy, and the southwest of Great Britain were worst affected. In many areas, temperatures were 18°F higher than normal. The temperature shot up to more than 118°F in some places.

Cracks in the bed of the dried up Rhine River in Germany

Warm, low rivers

The heat wave made water warm up and evaporate, reducing water levels. The low water levels prevented ships from moving up rivers across Europe. The warmer water killed fish and other wildlife that were used to cooler temperatures. The water was also too warm for some nuclear power plants to use. They closed down, causing power shortages.

Why did it happen?

Scientists worked out that global warming was four times more likely to have caused the 2003 heat wave than natural climate variation. Other parts of the world suffered extreme weather events at about the same time. For example, there were droughts in Australia and floods in the United States.

A plane drops water on a forest fire in Majorca, Spain.

Crops and fires

Large areas of crops died in the heat, and European farmers produced one tenth less wheat than usual. Many wild plants became very dry, and wildfires were a big problem. One tenth of Portuguese forests burned down in the heat wave.

Sago Mine lightning strike

The power of lightning from storm clouds can be lethal when it hits people directly. It can also cause major damage when sparks start fires or explosions—especially in hard-to-reach places, such as underground mines.

The tragedy strikes

Sago coal mine in West Virginia reopened on January 2, 2006 after shutting down for the New Year holiday. Two carts of miners trundled down into the mine to begin work as usual just after 6:00 a.m. At 6:30 a.m., there was an explosion that caved in part of the mine. The miners in the second cart escaped, but 13 miners in the first cart were trapped. Only one survived. The others died from breathing poisonous gas.

Top Facts

- In the United States, the chance of someone being struck by lightning is 1 in 230,000. There is a one in three chance the lightning will kill them when it strikes.

- Airplanes are struck by lightning about twice a year, but they are designed to protect the passengers inside by having a separate metal skin on the outside.

Where it happened

Sago is a remote mining community in the Appalachian Mountains in West Virginia. It is a tiny place with about 35 residents—even the nearest big town, Buckhannon, only has a population of 8,000 people. Lightning is a common event in this area, although Florida to the south is the state where lightning strikes occur most frequently.

Mine fires

Fires in coal mines are a major problem worldwide. Although there may be a lot of processing equipment on the surface of a mine, most of the mine itself is far below ground and can be very inaccessible in an emergency. Methane explosions can set alight coal, which then slowly burns. Firefighters cannot easily put out these fires because the fuel is too deep and difficult to reach. They sometimes pump sludge down shafts to cool the coal.

Processing equipment above ground at the Sago Mine

Ignition

The explosion at Sago was probably caused by a lightning strike at the surface that set fire to methane gas inside the mine. Meteorologists recorded 100 lightning strikes in the region within 40 minutes of the explosion. Methane gas naturally forms underground in rocks alongside coal. Fans and pumps are used to remove methane from mines, but at Sago the gas had built up during the shut down.

It's Amazing!

Lightning does strike twice in the same place! The Empire State Building in New York City is struck by lightning about 100 times each year. Once, it was struck 15 times in 15 minutes!

Rescue operation

The miners were trapped almost 2 miles down. Rescuers had to wear special breathing equipment and avoid making any sparks that could cause another explosion. The families did not learn the trapped miners had died until January 4.

Rescue workers prepare to go down into the Sago Mine.

El Niño in Peru

El Niño climate events happen every few years, but in 1997–98 the conditions were among the worst in the 20th century. Peru was particularly severely affected by this El Niño.

Ocean change

Winds normally blow surface water from the Pacific Ocean westward from the coast of Peru. Cold water rises to the surface to take its place. In 1997–98, this pattern reversed, and warm water moved toward Peru. This raised water and air temperatures above normal levels. It also brought heavy rain as warm, humid air met colder air, causing floods and mud slides.

The fishing fleet in Callao, Peru, was unused during El Niño.

Top Facts

- Around the world, the 1997–98 El Niño event caused damage that cost about 40 billion dollars.

- Fresh water from the floods ran into the ocean and made it less salty than usual. This contributed to the lower than normal fish stocks off the coast of Peru.

ECUADOR

PERU

Callao •

Pacific Ocean

Where it happened

In 1997–98, the devastation caused by El Niño began in Peru and Ecuador, then spread across the globe. Places affected included Southeast Asia, where there were droughts and wildfires, the United States, which had mud slides, and Europe, where there were floods.

Highly humid

High ocean-surface temperatures during El Niño in 1997–98 caused a lot of sea water to evaporate into water vapor, creating high humidity. Satellite sensors detected unusually high amounts of water vapor in the atmosphere above the eastern Pacific Ocean.

Satellite image showing humidity in the Pacific Ocean, February 1998

Pacific Ocean

Red areas show high humidity.

It's Amazing!

The lower numbers of fish in the eastern Pacific affected food chains. There were fewer seabirds, sea lions, and whales, all of which feed on animals in the cold waters off Peru.

Disappearing fish

One of Peru's biggest exports is fishmeal, made from anchovies and sardines. These fish usually arrive in the waters off Peru in December to feed on the animals that thrive in the cold water. During El Niño, the fish went elsewhere because the water was too warm. In the first five months of 1998, Peruvian fishermen caught less than 20 percent of the usual amount of fish.

People try to cross a flooded river in Peru during the 1997–98 El Niño.

The economy

El Niño affected the jobs of over half a million Peruvians at a cost of more than 2 billion dollars. It devastated the country's rural economy. As rivers broke their banks, farmland was flooded and villages washed away.

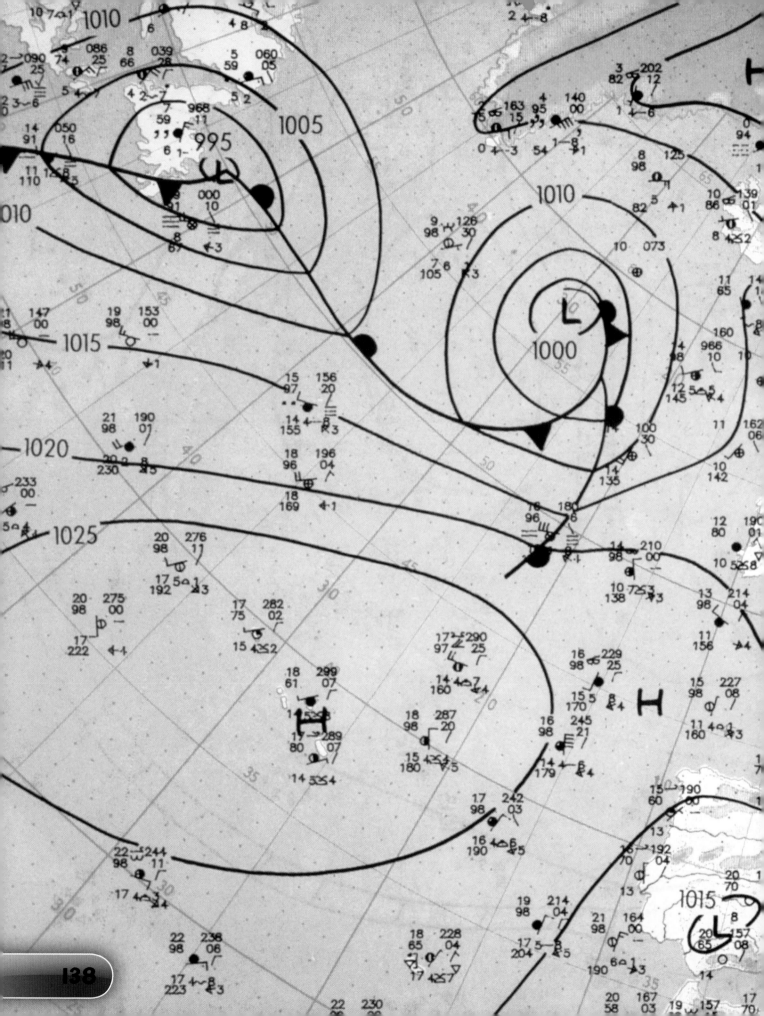

WEATHER FORECASTS

We are used to watching weather reports on the television or reading the newspaper to find out what tomorrow's weather will be like. But weather forecasts are a fairly recent invention. Years ago, people relied on observing nature and on wisdom handed down through the generations to predict the weather. Meteorologists today use amazing technology to produce forecasts, but some of the old sayings are still true.

Predicting the weather

You need to know what the weather is going to be like if you want to play a sport, go on vacation, or do some gardening. Meteorologists are scientists whose job it is to forecast, or predict, the weather using computers and modern technology.

Weather and jobs

Getting an accurate weather forecast is essential for many people. For example, farmers need rain to grow their crops but dry weather for harvesting them, and fishermen need to know if the sea will be calm when they go out in their boats.

It's Amazing!

Some weather wisdom is a little strange. For example, people used to believe that it would snow if a cat washed behind both its ears!

A snowboarder in the Alps in Switzerland

Enjoying the weather

Weather forecasts are also important for people during their leisure time. They may want hot, sunny days when they go on vacation to a beach or a lot of snow for skiing. Many sporting events rely on good weather, which is why a lot of sports are played in the summer.

A pinecone opens.

Plants and animals

In the past, people watched nature to help forecast the weather. For example, they worked out that some types of winged ants fly from their nests before summer storms, and that pinecones open in dry weather and close in wet weather.

Early forecasts

Some of the earliest forecasts were made in about 650 BC by the Babylonians from Mesopotamia (present-day Iraq). They watched cloud patterns to predict the weather. They also believed that studying the stars and planets helped them forecast the weather.

Wheat is harvested on a dry, sunny day.

Power surges

Weather affects how much energy we use. For example, in cold weather, people heat their homes more. Power companies have to store extra fuel when there are surges, or high demands, in power use. This is why forecasts are vital for power companies.

Faster forecasting

Before the invention of the telegraph in 1837, there was no quick way to tell people that bad weather was on its way. The telegraph allowed people to send messages about the weather down wires using electrical signals. This meant people in different places could share weather observations almost instantly for the first time. Since then, many inventions have made meteorology more accurate and faster. For example, computers can process vast amounts of weather data in a second.

Heating increases fuel demand in cold weather.

Measuring weather

Meteorologists all over the world use the same type of instruments to measure weather. This ensures that weather readings are accurate and can easily be compared. Meteorologists take readings several times a day to get a picture of how the weather is changing.

Temperature

Thermometers are devices that measure the temperature. The earliest thermometers were made in the 16th century and were simple glass straws filled with water. Liquids expand as they heat up and contract as they cool, so the water moved up or down the tube to show changes in temperature. Today, most meteorologists use thermometers with liquid mercury inside instead of water.

A sunshine recorder

Sun's brightness

The brightness of the sun is measured with a sunshine recorder. This has a glass sphere that focuses sunlight and burns a mark on card. As the sun moves across the sky, the burn mark moves along the strip of cardboard placed behind the glass sphere.

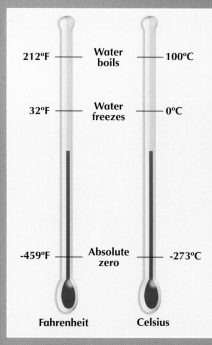

212°F	Water boils	100°C
32°F	Water freezes	0°C
-459°F	Absolute zero	-273°C
Fahrenheit		Celsius

Temperature units

The two main units for measuring temperature are Fahrenheit and Celsius. In the Fahrenheit scale, 32 degrees is the freezing point of water and 212 is the boiling point of water. In the Celsius scale, 0 degrees is the freezing point of water and 100 degrees is the boiling point of water.

It's Amazing!

Absolute zero is the temperature at which scientists believe nothing else could be colder. This temperature is -459 degrees Fahrenheit or -273 degrees Celsius.

Wind measurements

Anemometers measure wind speed using small cups attached to a spindle. The stronger the wind, the faster the cups turn the spindle. Weather vanes show the wind direction. They are often shaped like an arrow with the pointed end showing where the wind is coming from. Wind socks are cloth bags that fill with wind, showing the wind's strength and direction.

Cup

Anemometer

Spindle

Humidity

Humidity, or the amount of moisture in the air, is measured with a psychrometer. This contains two thermometers, one of which has a wet cloth around it. The lower the humidity, the faster the water in the cloth evaporates and cools the thermometer. High humidity cools it less. The wet thermometer will usually record a lower temperature than the other thermometer. The difference between the two temperatures is used to work out the humidity.

Morning dew forms on a blade of grass.

Make an anemometer

- Ask an adult to bend a wire coat hanger into a square shape.

- On the top inside edge, tape on a square of thin cardboard slightly smaller than the square coat hanger so it can flap up and down.

- Hang up your simple anemometer outside and watch how the cardboard swings higher, the faster the wind blows.

Pressure and precipitation

To get a complete picture of the weather, meteorologists need to measure precipitation and air pressure. Precipitation is the actual rain or snowfall in a place. Air pressure tells them how wet and windy or dry and calm the weather will be in the next few days.

Pressing down

Air pressure is the push of air against the ground. The pressure varies depending on whether the air is rising or sinking. Low pressure often brings stormy weather, whereas high pressure often brings calm weather. Meteorologists measure pressure using an instrument called a barometer.

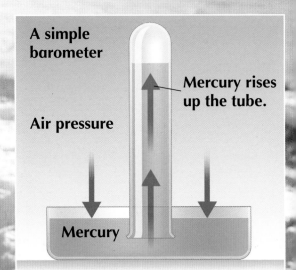

A simple barometer

Air pressure

Mercury rises up the tube.

Mercury

Mercury barometer

Some barometers have a tube containing a column of mercury that moves with changing pressure. The higher the pressure, the farther the mercury rises in the tube. The pressure is often read in millimeters.

Gauges used in places where it often snows sometimes have heaters to melt the snow.

Rain gauges in the Pennines, Great Britain

Make a barometer

- Stick a see-through drinking straw against a ruler and put them inside a jar one-third full of water.

- Suck water halfway up the straw, then put modeling clay over the end to seal it. Mark the water level on the straw.

- Note the level of water in the straw each day and see how it moves as the air pressure changes.

Snow depth

Meteorologists measure the depth of snow with a ruler in inches or millimeters. They collect the snow on a snow board, which is placed on the ground. It is easier to measure the snow on a flat board than on bumpy ground, where the snow depth will vary. The board is painted white, so it reflects any heat to prevent the snow from melting before it is measured.

Deep snow at this ski resort in France has covered these cars and made driving impossible.

It's Amazing!

The lowest air pressure on Earth is found in the center of hurricanes and tornadoes. It is no surprise that the winds in these extreme storms are the fastest on the planet.

Rain catcher

Meteorologists often use a standard rain gauge to measure the amount of rain accurately. This is a funnel attached to a narrow measuring tube, marked in inches or millimeters. The rain falls into the funnel and flows into the tube. The mouth of the funnel has an area that is 10 times that of the tube. This means that a depth of 10 inches of rain in the tube gives a reading of 1 inch of actual rainfall.

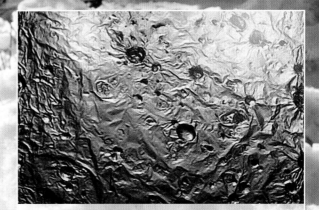

Hail pads

Meteorologists use hail pads to record the size of hailstones. A hail pad is a foam pad coated with foil. The hail dents the pad when it falls—the bigger the hailstones, the larger the dents.

On land and sea

Meteorologists measure the weather at many different points on Earth. They often keep their instruments in weather stations, which they visit regularly to record weather data. Some weather stations send data automatically.

Recording the weather

Weather stations are set up at many fixed positions around the globe at ground level. They record climate in places all around the world, including deserts, rainforests, cities, mountains, and at sea. In frozen climates, such as in Antarctica, special instruments are sometimes used because the mercury in thermometers and barometers can freeze.

WMO

The World Meteorological Organization (WMO) was set up in 1951 to make sure that meteorologists use standard equipment, so that they get standard measurements. It encourages meteorologists to work together.

It's Amazing!

When meteorologists put a rain gauge at the airport in Seattle, they did not know they had chosen the driest place in the city. The average yearly rainfall for the city is 10 inches more than at the airport.

A meteorologist takes readings from instruments inside a vented box.

The weather station

A basic weather station has an anemometer and a weather vane mounted on a post, plus a rain gauge. A thermometer, psychrometer, and barometer are kept in a special vented box. The box shelters the instruments from precipitation, sunshine, and wind, which may cause them to give false readings.

Automatic weather stations

In remote places, automatic stations record the weather and the data is then sent via satellite to computers, which store the information. Some of these weather stations have self-emptying rain gauges, and operate using solar power.

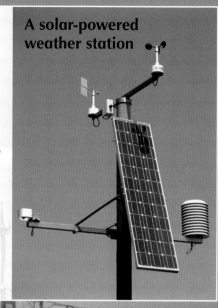

A solar-powered weather station

Floating stations

Weather ships are dedicated to recording the weather, ocean currents, and sea temperatures full time. More than 3,500 other ships from 53 nations also help by taking measurements. Some mini weather stations are even mounted on floating buoys. Meteorologists track their movement on ocean currents using satellites (see page 153).

A meteorologist checks a weather station in Antarctica.

Ocean structures

Weather stations are also set up on secured ocean structures, including lighthouses and oil platforms. The data they record is used to provide early warnings of weather conditions that could endanger crews working on ships and oil platforms.

Weather in the sky

The weather that affects our lives happens on the ground, but much of it starts in the atmosphere high above us. Meteorologists use weather balloons and aircraft to measure the weather in the atmosphere so they can forecast the world's climate more accurately.

The walls of a hurricane's eye seen from an aircraft

Flying into weather

Powerful winds high in the atmosphere, including the jet streams, influence the movement of air around the globe. Low temperatures high up may change water vapor into hail or intense rain. Instruments on the outside of weather airplanes record wind speed, temperature, humidity, and other data in the atmosphere. Observers inside the planes can see clouds close up and even fly into hurricanes.

The first balloons

Balloons have been used to monitor the weather for more than 200 years. In 1783, hot-air balloon pioneers the Montgolfier brothers released a small weather balloon to watch how it blew in the wind before allowing passengers to board their hot-air balloon. Since the 19th century, meteorologists have used small weather balloons to measure wind speed. Radiosondes (see opposite) were first used to explore the upper atmosphere in the 20th century.

Weather on Venus

Weather balloons are not just used on the earth. In 1985, a Soviet space expedition used a space probe called Vega 2 to measure the atmosphere on the planet Venus. A tough balloon suspended Vega 2 at about 30 miles above the surface of the planet. It recorded powerful winds, similar pressure to the Earth's surface, and tropical temperatures.

The planet Venus

Weather balloons

Taking flights to observe the weather is expensive and can be dangerous. Instead, most meteorologists use unmanned weather balloons. These balloons carry a measuring device called a radiosonde, which transmits weather data back to the ground using radio signals. The balloons usually burst after a few hours, and the radiosonde parachutes back to the ground. Computers track how fast weather balloons travel to work out wind speeds.

Weather balloons are filled with hydrogen gas, which is lighter than air.

It's Amazing!

There are 1,100 radiosonde launch sites worldwide. Meteorologists launch weather balloons from these sites at exactly the same time, twice a day. The radiosondes reveal a snapshot of the weather across the planet.

Different balloons

Meteorologists use bigger, tougher balloons to go higher in the atmosphere. For example, a 28-ounce balloon will burst about 20 miles above the ground, but a heavier one can go higher.

This is your captain...

Weather instruments have been used on board aircraft for more than 50 years. Today, computers on the ground automatically receive daily weather data from commercial aircraft. These aircraft include passenger airliners on routine flights and military aircraft on training missions to more remote areas.

A U.S. Air Force WC-130 weather-monitoring aircraft

U.S. AIR FORCE

149

Radars

Meteorologists use radars to form pictures of the weather in the atmosphere. These machines send out waves of energy, called microwaves, that bounce back when they hit rain and snow. Radars use these echoes to work out where the precipitation is and how fast storms are moving.

How radar works

Weather radars have two main parts. The transmitter sends out short, controlled pulses of microwaves into the air. These pulses spread out as they travel, covering a wider and wider area. When the waves hit raindrops, for example, part of the pulse is echoed back. The receiver is the part of the radar that records the echo. The longer the gap between a pulse and its echo, the farther away the object is.

A radar image shows a storm over Kansas.

Rainy days

Weather radars can show how much rain falls on an area in a day. The radar produces an image that colors the area according to the amount of rain in millimeters. In this example, the red areas have had more rain than the blue areas.

Weather radar stations like this one in Germany are often located on high ground.

Radar screens

The echoes that radars receive back from rain and other precipitation are sent to a computer. The computer processes the data and produces a map of the weather, which is viewed on a television screen. The map shows the type of precipitation, how much is falling, and how fast the weather system is traveling. Meteorologists use this information to work out when storms may hit and when to warn people about severe weather.

Lightning sensors

Lightning produces radio waves, which spread out like the ripples on a pond. The waves can be detected using a network of special aerials called lightning sensors. Computers use data from the sensors to pinpoint the location of the lightning.

A tornado rages over Florida, USA.

Tornado speeds

Tornadoes show up as hook-shaped echoes on radar screens. The shape is caused by the rain clouds swirling fast around the center of the storm. Radars can help forecasters give vital early warnings of tornadoes.

Weather at war

During World War II, military operators watching radar screens could not always get clear echoes from moving objects, such as planes and ships. They realized that "busy" echoes happened when it was raining. Scientists went on to develop weather radars after the war.

Space sensors

Cameras and other instruments carried into space on satellites and spacecraft tell us a lot about the weather. They produce amazing images of our weather—from hurricanes and snow to sandstorms and smoke from wildfires.

Weather satellites

Weather satellites carry weather-sensing instruments into space. The instruments are powered by solar panels. High-resolution cameras feed images of cloud cover to computers on the ground using radio transmitters. These images are used to track and predict weather systems and wind movement.

A satellite image shows Hurricane Ivan in 2004.

Tracking storms

Satellite images show the size, speed, and rate of growth of tropical storms, which develop far out at sea. These photographs reveal the beautiful but deadly spiral of clouds above a hurricane.

Tiros I

The first weather satellite to capture reliable images of weather was called *Tiros I*. It was launched on April 1, 1960 and operated for 78 days. It carried television cameras and sent television pictures of weather systems back to the ground.

Seeing heat

Scanning radiometers on weather satellites detect heat given off by Earth. Computers convert this data into color-coded maps showing the humidity or temperature of Earth. The maps help meteorologists to predict where weather systems may form. For example, hurricanes form over warm water.

A radiometer map of ocean temperatures. The orange areas are warmer than the blue areas.

A GOES satellite used for monitoring the weather

Getting up there

Satellites are carried into space by rockets or space shuttles. They remain in orbit because, although the planet's gravity pulls them toward it, their engines can push them away if they fall too close to the atmosphere. Some satellites are geostationary—they orbit along the equator at the same speed as the planet rotates. Others pass north or south over the poles twice a day.

A tornado's path

Weather satellites orbit at up to 22,000 miles above the surface. Powerful digital cameras with zoom lenses can pick out the paths of destruction left by tornadoes. They can even identify the neighborhoods and streets where damage was worst.

Path of tornado in Maryland

From weather data to forecasts

A lot of data is recorded by weather stations, satellites, radar, and radiosondes every day. Computers combine this with data about climate and weather patterns so that meteorologists can produce weather forecasts.

Creating forecasts

The global weather data is sent via a huge computer network to meteorologists around the world. Weather forecasters in every country take the data they need to make their own local forecasts. Forecasts for up to six days ahead are the most accurate. Predicting the weather over longer periods is more difficult.

A satellite image of the San Francisco Bay, California, shows the city in gray and vegetation in red.

Ground effects

To forecast accurately, meteorologists must take into account the surface features, or topography, of an area. For example, an urban area will be warmer than the surrounding countryside because the buildings in city centers store heat.

Weather data is displayed on monitors at a meteorological center in the United States.

Special forecasts

Meteorologists sometimes create special forecasts for businesses. For example, supermarkets may buy a lot of ice cream, ice, and cool drinks if a heat wave is forecast and clothes stores may stock up on warm, waterproof clothing if wintery weather is on its way.

Computer models

Powerful computers are used to create forecasting models. These are computer simulations of what the weather will be like in the future. Current weather data is fed into a computer and compared with past climate records. The computer then produces a model of what the weather will be like in the next six days.

Observing the current weather conditions helps forecasters make accurate nowcasts.

Nowcasting

"Nowcasting" is the word used to describe forecasting weather in the next six hours or less. In this short period, there is often not enough data for accurate forecasts. A forecaster with knowledge of local weather patterns and topography, who can observe the current weather, will usually nowcast more accurately than a computer.

Top Facts

- Computer models divide the globe into 55-mile squares, or grid points. At each point, readings are taken throughout the atmosphere to work out how the weather is behaving.

- The models predict what the weather will be like at 15-minute intervals in the future.

Weather maps and symbols

Forecasters make charts of the weather for their region. By comparing charts taken at different times, they can produce weather forecasts for the public on television or in newspapers.

Synoptic charts

Meteorologists take the data from weather stations and create synoptic charts to help them forecast the weather. Each weather station is represented on the chart by a standard symbol, or plot, with numbers around it that sum up the weather at a station at a given time. Plots always show precipitation, cloud cover, sunshine, wind, humidity, and temperature in the same way.

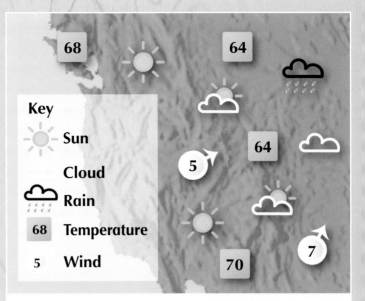

Key
- ☀ Sun
- ☁ Cloud
- 🌧 Rain
- 68 Temperature
- 5 Wind

Forecasts for the public

To make forecasts easier for ordinary people to understand, meteorologists use familiar symbols. For example, precipitation is shown as a cloud shape with raindrops or snowflakes. Sunny weather is shown as a sun with rays. Numbers give the temperature and wind speed.

Forecasters analyze the patterns formed by isobars to work out how air masses of different pressure are moving across a region.

Weather lines

Meteorologists draw lines on the synoptic charts between points with the same atmospheric pressure. These are known as isobars and show areas of high and low pressure. Since winds blow from areas of high to low pressure, isobars tell meteorologists about wind strength and direction.

Television maps

The first television weather presenters in 1936 drew weather maps by hand with wax crayons! Later, they used magnetic symbols and satellite maps. Today, some television stations have given up weather symbols for maps that use virtual reality technology to produce realistic looking weather effects.

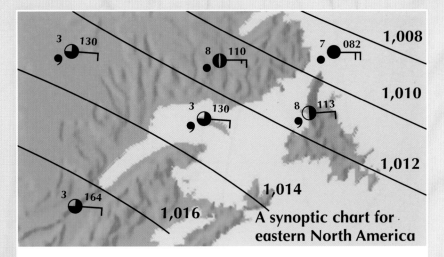

A synoptic chart for eastern North America

Joining the plots

Each weather station is represented on a synoptic chart by a plot symbol that describes the weather in that particular location (see the chart below for an explanation of the symbols). The lines across the chart are the isobars, and the pressure in millibars is written next to each isobar.

Reading plot symbols

A plot is shown as a circle. How much of the circle is filled in represents the cloud cover. This is measured in oktas, with eight oktas indicating complete cloud cover. A line sticking out of the plot circle like a tail points in the direction the wind is blowing, and the number of lines on the tail shows wind speed. Dots, stars, triangles, and lines around the plot show the precipitation. Numbers next to the plot give the temperature, humidity, and pressure readings.

STANDARD SYMBOLS USED ON WEATHER CHARTS

SYMBOL	PRECIPITATION	SYMBOL	CLOUD COVER	SYMBOL	WIND SPEED
🌧	DRIZZLE	○	CLEAR SKY	◎	CALM
▽	SHOWER	◐	1 OKTAS	○—	1–2 KNOTS
●	RAIN	◔	2 OKTAS	○⌐	5 KNOTS
★	SNOW	◕	3 OKTAS	○⌐	10 KNOTS
△	HAIL	◑	4 OKTAS	○⌐	15 KNOTS
⎘	THUNDER	◒	5 OKTAS	○⌐	20 KNOTS
∴	HEAVY RAIN	◕	6 OKTAS	○▼	50 KNOTS +
✶	SLEET	◖	7 OKTAS		
✳	SNOW	●	8 OKTAS		
≡	MIST	⊗	SKY OBSCURED		
≣	FOG				

Weather fronts and systems

Air masses of different temperature and humidity move through the atmosphere. Where the air masses meet is known as a front. Meteorologists focus on fronts because these create typical patterns of weather, or weather systems, such as cyclones and anticyclones.

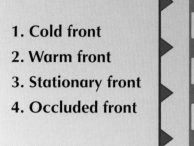

1. Cold front
2. Warm front
3. Stationary front
4. Occluded front

1 2 3 4

Front symbols

Meteorologists use lines with triangles and semicircles on them to represent fronts on weather maps and charts. The triangles and semicircles point in the direction that the front is moving.

Weather fronts

Air masses have different temperatures and pressure, so they do not mix. When they meet, warm air rises up over cooler air. A warm front is where a warm air mass crashes into a cold air mass. A cold front is where a cold air mass crashes into a warm air mass. An occluded front is when a fast-moving cold front catches up with a warm front and merges with it. A stationary front happens when two air masses meet, but neither is strong enough to replace the other.

Battle front

The term "front" was first used to describe the weather in the 1920s by Norwegian scientists, who compared two air masses colliding to two armies as they clash on the battle front. Just like one army defeating another in a battle, one air mass ultimately takes over, pushing the other one out of the way.

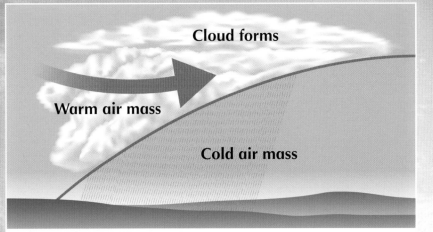

Cloud forms

Warm air mass

Cold air mass

At a warm front

A warm front happens when a warm air mass meets a cold air mass and gradually rises over the long wedge of cold air. Clouds slowly build up over a large area of the sky. Warm fronts often bring long periods of rain and drizzle, but they are usually followed by warmer temperatures when the front has passed by.

Weather systems

The angle, speed, and direction at which air masses clash affect the weather systems they produce. Some produce areas of low pressure, called "cyclones" or "depressions." Other air masses produce areas of high pressure, known as "anticyclones." Winds spiral into a depression, bringing rain clouds. They spiral out of an anticyclone bringing calmer weather. Cyclones often result in extreme weather, such as hurricanes and typhoons.

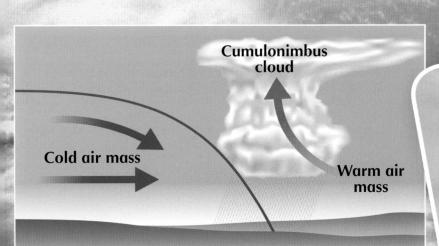

Cumulonimbus cloud

Cold air mass

Warm air mass

At a cold front

At a cold front, higher-pressure cold air cuts underneath warm air, forcing it up fast and at a much steeper angle than in a warm front. The humid, warm air forms a narrow band of thick cumulonimbus clouds, which bring a short burst of heavy precipitation and blustery winds. This is usually followed by cold, dry weather.

It's Amazing!

In the Northern Hemisphere, winds blow clockwise around an anticyclone, but in the Southern Hemisphere, they blow counterclockwise. This difference is the result of the planet's rotation dragging winds away from the equator.

Weather warnings

Forecasters alert people when weather is likely to be dangerous. They give warnings that inform people if there is severe weather on the way and advise them what to do.

Types of warning

Television and radio stations may give weather warnings as part of their usual weather forecasts. Shipping forecasts are descriptions of the weather and wave height at different points on the ocean used by sailors to avoid stormy weather. When hazardous weather, such as a tornado, is forecast, governments may use sirens and soldiers to make sure everyone knows of the danger.

First warnings

In 1870, the National Weather Service in the United States was the first to give weather warnings. Teams of soldiers recorded weather data and sent it to Washington, D.C., from where weather warnings were sent around the country.

A baseball stadium in Japan with a retractable roof

Events and locations

Major outdoor events are very dependent upon the weather conditions—bad weather can lead to cancellation. Some large venues have even been built with retractable roofs. That way, if there is a warning that bad weather is on its way, the roof can be closed and the event can continue.

Watches and warnings

Warnings are often given in stages. The first, early warning is called a watch. A flood watch means there are weather systems that will bring heavy rain in the next few days. It recommends that people should watch water levels in rivers and be prepared. When a warning is given, it means hazardous weather will strike in the next few hours.

Highways

Governments and companies that care for roads and traffic safety warn drivers about bad weather. They use road signs and flashing lights to warn road users about high winds, snow, fog, or heavy rain—all of which could make driving dangerous.

A road sign for snow.

A fishing vessel sails through rough water on the Bering Sea.

ACONA

It's Amazing!

Observing a storm can act as a weather warning. If the gap between lightning and thunder is less than 30 seconds, you should find shelter immediately and wait 30 minutes after the last thunder clap before leaving.

People evacuate before Hurricane Ivan hits the Cayman Islands, 2004.

Hurricane warnings

The stages of a hurricane warning in the United States are gale warning, tropical storm warning, and hurricane warning. Coast guards put up coded flags to warn boats about the conditions. People are warned to be prepared to evacuate their homes if necessary.

Weather sayings

Weather sayings may sound a bit silly, but many have some truth behind them. They are often based on observations of the weather, perhaps over many generations, passed on from parents to children in rhymes.

Weather lore

Many common weather sayings originate from observations of how the weather affects things. For example, people noticed that if the sky was red in the evening, the next day would be fine. They remembered this by saying, "Red sky at night, shepherd's delight." This rhyme is true—the sky looks red because dust particles, held in the air by an anticyclone (which brings fair weather), scatter blue light in sunlight, leaving just red light.

Hair humidity

There is a weather saying that rain is on the way if people with curly hair find their hair curlier. The saying is true—hair does contract, or shrink, in damp weather. In 1783, the Swiss scientist Horace-Bénédict de Saussure built a machine called a hygrometer that used the contraction of hair in wet weather to measure humidity. Similar machines are still used today.

A red sunset such as this is often a sign of good weather the next day.

A groundhog is a small mammal that hibernates through winter and wakes in the spring.

Groundhog Day

In the United States, some people believe that if on February 2, the groundhog sees its shadow, 30 days of winter remain. If not, they say, spring will follow immediately. In parts of the country, people gather on February 2 to see if the local groundhog, a type of rodent, will emerge from hibernation or return to its burrow.

Cow weather vanes

"A cow with its tail to the west, makes weather the best; a cow with its tail to the east, makes weather the least." This saying from the northeast USA has some truth. This is because, in that part of the world, east winds bring wet weather and west winds fair weather. Cows usually feed with their tails pointing to the wind.

Cows stand with their faces away from the wind.

True or false?

Sayings that predict the weather over a short period of time, often using observations of the sky or nature, can be fairly accurate. Sayings that try to predict the weather over longer periods, such as by watching groundhogs, are only ever right by chance.

Altocumulus clouds form a mackerel sky.

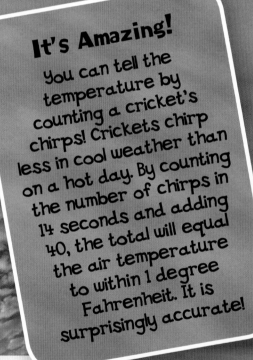

It's Amazing!

You can tell the temperature by counting a cricket's chirps! Crickets chirp less in cool weather than on a hot day. By counting the number of chirps in 14 seconds and adding 40, the total will equal the air temperature to within 1 degree Fahrenheit. It is surprisingly accurate!

Mackerel sky

"Mare's tails and mackerel scales make tall ships carry low sails." "Mare's tails" is a common name for cirrus clouds. They form high in the atmosphere. "Mackerel scales" are altocumulus clouds. Both these types of clouds develop before storms with high winds. In the past, tall ships lowered their sails to prevent the high winds damaging them.

WEATHER POWER

Weather alters our planet as dramatically as volcanoes and earthquakes do—but it takes a lot longer. Over many years, sunlight, wind, and moving water in rivers and oceans can damage and break up rocks. Rain and melting snow can wash them away, leaving transformed landscapes. The energy in weather is plentiful and free. Many inventions use this energy to power machinery or to produce electricity.

Weather and rocks

Energy from the Sun creates weather that not only affects but also changes Earth's surface. Wind, temperature, precipitation, and moving water in rivers and oceans can cause rocks to break up and blow or wash away—they can even change the structure of rocks.

Types of rock

Earth is made up of three types of rock. Igneous rocks form from molten (liquid) rock. They can soldify beneath the surface or can be thrown out by volcanoes. Metamorphic rocks are formed when old rocks are pushed below the surface and then squeezed and heated until they change their structure. Sometimes, metamorphic rocks are then pushed back to the surface. Sedimentary rocks are made up of tiny pieces of other rocks that have been broken up by the weather.

Top Facts

- Marble is a metamorphic rock. It wears away 20 times faster than granite, which is an extremely hard igneous rock.

Waves pound the coast of Cornwall, Great Britain.

It's Amazing!

About 75 percent of all rocks on the Earth's surface are either sedimentary rocks or metamorphic rocks.

Granite is a type of igneous rock.

Slate is a type of metamorphic rock.

Sandstone is a type of sedimentary rock.

Igneous, metamorphic, and sedimentary

Igneous rocks, such as granite, can be very hard. Sedimentary rocks, such as sandstone, usually have a crumbly texture because they are made up of tiny pieces of rock. Metamorphic rocks vary greatly in texture, and include smooth slate.

Sedimentary rock is formed from tiny pieces of other rocks.

Igneous rock is formed when other rocks are pushed into the earth and melted.

Metamorphic rock is formed when other rocks are squeezed and heated underground.

The rock cycle

The rock cycle explains the way rocks form and how one type of rock is changed into another type. For example, igneous rocks are broken up by the action of the wind, sea, and rivers. The tiny pieces of igneous rock then collect on seabeds and flood plains and, over millions of years, these tiny particles are squeezed together to form sedimentary rocks.

Changing rocks

The breaking up of rocks by the wind, sea, and rivers is called weathering (see pages 168–169). For instance, weathering can break up the rock mineral calcite into tiny pieces. These pieces dissolve in water and help to form calcium carbonate, which is later deposited to form the sedimentary rock limestone. Limestone can then be heated and squeezed underground and changed into the metamorphic rock marble.

Rock layers

The tiny pieces of stone that make up sedimentary rocks slowly build up into layers, which are called strata. Over time, new layers are laid down on top of the old layers, which are squashed together to form new rock.

Sedimentary rock set down in layers in the Painted Desert, Arizona

Weathering has worn away this statue in Bali, Indonesia.

Stone weathering

Weathering can take from tens to thousands of years, depending on how hard the rocks are. Softer rocks wear away more quickly. You can see the effects of weathering on statues. Old carvings on statues are more worn away than those on newer ones.

Weathering

Extremes of temperature can cause rock to break up into small pieces. The chemicals in rainwater can also react with rock, making it turn soft and crumbly. These effects are known as weathering.

Physical weathering

The type of weathering that happens because of temperature changes is called physical weathering. The rocks break up into smaller and smaller particles. Bacteria and plants start to live and grow among these particles and these later die and rot, or break down. The tiny particles of rock and remains of plants and animals mix together to form soil.

A shaft of light falls into a cave near Valladolid, Mexico.

Splitting rocks

Exfoliation occurs when the surface layers of rocks break away like the layers of an onion. During the day, the rocks heat up and expand, and during the night, they cool and contract. This puts pressure on the tiny gaps between layers, causing the surface layers to peel off.

Heat and cold have caused this rock on Kilimanjaro, Africa, to exfoliate.

Top Facts

- Biological weathering is when living things break up rocks. Growing plant roots, for example, force open cracks in rocks.

- It may take 100 to 1000 years for about $1/2$ inch of soil to form as a result of weathering.

Chemical weathering

Chemical weathering happens when chemicals dissolved in rainwater get into the ground and react with the minerals that make up the rock. These chemicals can change the mineral and make it crumbly. For example, the gas carbon dioxide dissolves in rainwater. When this rain hits limestone, it dissolves the rock and creates holes in the ground and even caves.

Cave features

As rainwater and streams dissolve limestone, they create sinkholes, which sink into the ground. Caves are formed when the water collects to form underground lakes and rivers, which dissolve more limestone. Stalactites and stalagmites are formed by water containing lime dripping from the cave roof. The water evaporates, leaving the lime behind, which builds up to form the stalactites and stalagmites.

Sinkhole

Limestone

Stalactite

Cave

Stalagmite

Underground lake

Erosion

Erosion is the movement of weathered rock or soil away from where it formed. Water in rivers and seas as well as the wind can carry pieces of weathered rock over great distances. For example, the strong winds in a sandstorm can carry sand particles hundreds of miles from their original location.

Weather and the rate of erosion

Extreme weather events can speed up the rate of erosion. Powerful winds can carry larger pieces of rock and stone (see page 178) than weaker winds. They can also create powerful ocean waves to wash away the sand on beaches and rocks near cliffs. Heavy rains will increase the flow of rivers and streams so that they carry away more soil and rocks, creating deep channels and gorges.

Testing erosion

- Put a mound of water-base clay on a tray and press some coins and stones into its surface.

- Spray water on the surface of the clay. Watch as the water changes color and washes away some of the clay.

- Repeat every day for a week. See how the clay under the coins and stones erodes slower than the exposed areas, just as exposed soft rocks erode quicker than those covered with harder stone.

Waterfalls

Sometimes, rivers flow over different types of rock. If one of these rocks is softer than the other, it will be eroded at a faster rate. This will create a sudden drop in the river where the river flows from the harder rock to the softer rock. This drop is called a waterfall.

Iguaçu Falls lie on the border between Brazil and Argentina.

Deposition

The Grand Canyon in Arizona is a deep gorge cut into the rock by the Colorado River.

When the energy levels of wind, sea, and rivers decrease, they deposit, or drop, the sand and rock particles they were carrying. For example, when a river flood dies down, it leaves behind the mud and sand it was carrying on the flooded ground. This creates a large, flat area of deposited mud called a floodplain.

It's Amazing!

The Huang He River in China erodes so much material that about 1.5 billion tons of sediment are deposited in the Yellow Sea every single year.

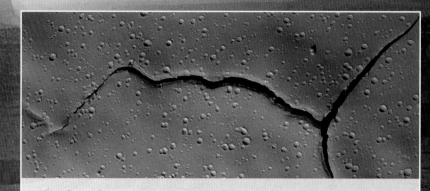

Splash power

Heavy raindrops act like tiny bombs when they hit the ground and may push sand or dust-size particles several inches out of the way. This is called splash erosion. During long storms, especially those that cause floods, particles can be carried much longer distances.

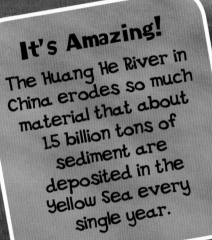

Uluru, or Ayers Rock, is found in the middle of Australia.

Exposed rocks

Sometimes, weathering and erosion of softer rock can leave hard rock exposed and sticking out of the ground. Uluru, or Ayers Rock, in Australia is a giant rock of hard sandstone that has not eroded as much as the softer sandstone around it.

Glaciers on the move

Moving ice is a major cause of erosion in cold climates. Ice creeps across the land, especially down mountain slopes, in massive sheets of ice called glaciers. The ice carries rocks with it that slowly erode the land. Many parts of the world that were once much colder than they are today have land forms that were created by glaciers.

How glaciers form

Glaciers start as snow falling on freezing land. The snow builds up in thick layers, especially in dips or valleys, because it is too cold to melt. Snow in the bottom layers is squeezed so hard that it changes into solid ice. Over many years, the ice builds up to form a glacier several hundred feet deep. The force of gravity on thousands of tons of ice makes it move slowly downhill.

The Pasterze Glacier in Austria

It's Amazing!

The ice in some glaciers moves fast because they are on steep slopes. The fastest glacier in the world is in Greenland. It is moving about 1.5 yards every hour.

A U-shaped valley carved by a glacier in Russia

Giant scouring pads

The rocks stuck to the bottom of a glacier can make it act like a giant scouring pad. They gradually rub away the ground underneath the glacier, gouging out a U-shaped valley. You can see a place where a glacier used to be by the shape of the valley left behind.

Make a mini glacier

- Put some sand in an ice-cube tray and add some water. Then freeze the water to make sandy ice cubes.

- Take a cube and rub one of the sandy sides over a flattened piece of modeling clay.

- You should see that the sand scratches the clay, and that some sand is left on the clay as the ice melts. This is similar to the way a glacier scrapes at the ground and deposits rocks.

Mystery rocks

Large boulders may be dragged or carried long distances by a glacier. After the glacier melts, these rocks, which are called "erratics," are deposited and left behind. Erratics are usually very different from other the rocks around them. They may be perched in unusual places, such as on hilltops.

Terminal moraine left by a glacier in Alaska

Moraines

A moraine is a collection of rocks that is left behind by a glacier. A terminal moraine is a line of rocks that forms at the front of a glacier. These rocks are pushed along by the glacier and then left behind in a line when the glacier melts.

Ice gain and loss

The upper part of a glacier will gain ice as more snow falls on it. The lower part, where it is warmer, will lose ice as it melts. If the amount of ice gained and the amount of ice lost are about the same, the glacier will stay the same size. If not, the glacier will grow or shrink.

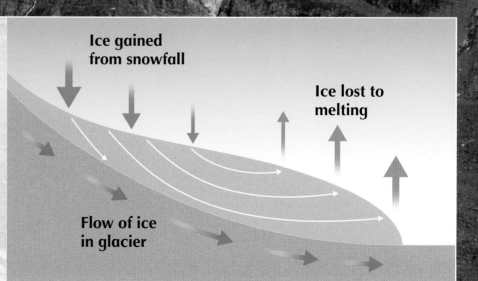

Ice gained from snowfall

Ice lost to melting

Flow of ice in glacier

Coasts under attack

Coastlines around the world are under constant attack from the sea. Waves pound the rock, breaking pieces off and creating beaches and other coastal features.

Wave force

In severe storms, waves grow huge, and can shift rocks weighing many hundreds of tons. Smaller waves pounding on the shore break apart rocks by forcing air into any cracks and splitting them open. Waves erode so much of the base that eventually the overhang falls off.

Top Facts

- Coastal erosion happens faster and affects larger areas when severe weather, such as hurricanes, batters coastlines.

- Erosion is also made worse when people dig up the seabed to make harbors. Lowering the seabed can also make waves hit the coasts harder.

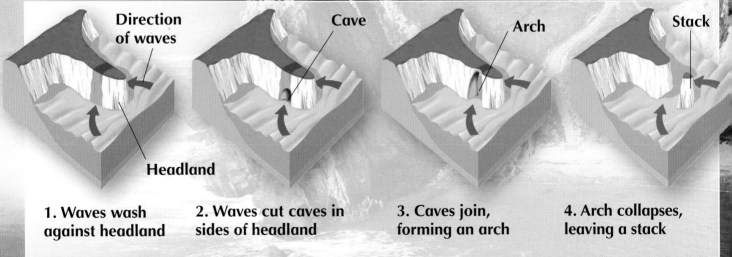

1. Waves wash against headland

2. Waves cut caves in sides of headland

3. Caves join, forming an arch

4. Arch collapses, leaving a stack

Arches and stacks

Coastal weathering can cause sea caves to form on either side of a headland. Arches are created when the caves meet, and weathering makes them get bigger. Often the power of the waves and the weight of unsupported rock in the middle of arches causes them to collapse. Stacks are the pillars of rock near cliffs that are left behind by fallen arches.

Sea cliffs tower over the coast near Lulworth, Dorset, Great Britain.

Bays and headlands

Different parts of coastlines wear away faster than others, depending on the type of rock. Bays are scooped out of coastlines where the rock is soft. Headlands are made of harder rock and jut out.

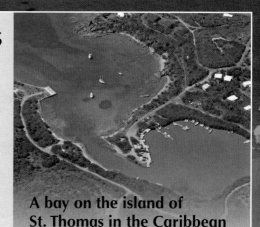

A bay on the island of St. Thomas in the Caribbean

Making sand

Weathered rocks carried in the sea grind together and bash into coastal cliffs. This action causes more weathering and turns some rock pieces into smooth pebbles. Other rock pieces are ground into sand and silt, which are deposited on parts of the coast, forming beaches and large boggy areas called mudflats.

It's Amazing!

Rising sea levels are increasing coastal erosion. Scientists predict that the coastline of the United States will lose about 1,500 buildings to the sea each year.

Groynes lie along a beach on the south coast of Great Britain.

Moving beaches

Waves hitting a beach at an angle wash sand and pebbles along it, depositing some but pulling some back into the sea, to be carried on to a different part of the beach. This is called "longshore drift." People sometimes build fences called groynes along beaches to trap the sand and pebbles.

River running

Rainwater and melting snow run off the land, forming streams and rivers. As the water flows to the ocean, it erodes rock and soil from the land, changing the shape of the landscape.

Top Facts

- In rainy seasons, whirlpools form in some rivers. These pick up rocks and erode round potholes in the riverbed.

- When a river creates a floodplain (see page 171), it deposits sand and silt that make the soil there very rich and good for farming.

River valleys

Rivers form on hills and in mountains. They cut down into the land as they flow, creating river valleys. A river starts at its source, such as a spring, and flows to its mouth, the point where the river meets the sea. This journey is called the river course.

Changing river valley

A river's ability to erode depends on how much water flows through it and where it is along its course. Near the river's source, when it is high above the river mouth, the river erodes down through the rock, creating steep V-shaped valleys. As the river moves through its middle and lower courses, it loses the energy to erode vertically. Instead, it erodes sideways, creating wide valleys and river bends, called meanders.

V-shaped valley of the upper course

A typical river course

Wider valley of the middle course

Wide, flat valley of the lower course

River source

Upper course

Middle course

Lower course

Meandering rivers

A meandering river moves more slowly and is wider than a river on higher ground. As the river flows, water moves faster on the inside of a meander than on the outside, eroding the bank. Around the outside of the bend, water moves more slowly so some mud is deposited and forms a river beach.

V-shaped valley created by the Daning River in China

It's Amazing!

The Huang He River in China flooded so severely in 1931 that more than 3.5 million people were killed—more than in any other flood.

Nile Delta

EGYPT

SAUDI ARABIA

Nile River

River deltas

When a river reaches its mouth, the energy of the sea slows the river down. The river spreads out and deposits mud and sand, forming a wide, fan-shaped area of small river channels called a delta. This satellite image shows the Nile Delta in Egypt, where the Nile River meets the Mediterranean Sea.

Oxbow lakes

As a river flows around a meander, it continues to erode the banks along the inside of the bend. Eventually, this blocks off the original bend, leaving behind a small lake, called an oxbow lake.

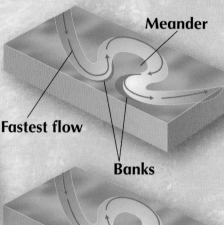

Meander

Fastest flow

Banks

Fastest flow

Erosion

River cuts across to follow straightest course

Oxbow lake remains

Wind erosion

The wind picks up sand and dust, and blasts it against rocks and other features. Jagged rocks are smoothed in the wind and others are carved into amazing shapes. Even sand itself is eroded until it turns to dust.

Sand power

Even the most powerful wind on the planet cannot weather rocks, unless it contains sand or dust. Sand is made up of particles, or grains, formed from a hard rock mineral called quartz. In windy weather, the sand bashes into and loosens more particles from rock surfaces. These are then blown away.

Balanced rock

Sometimes wind and sand can carve odd shapes. Balanced Rock in Utah is a huge rock that is the size of three school buses and rests on a narrow column. The base is thinner than the top because most wind erosion happens near to the ground.

Balanced Rock is in the Arches National Park in Utah.

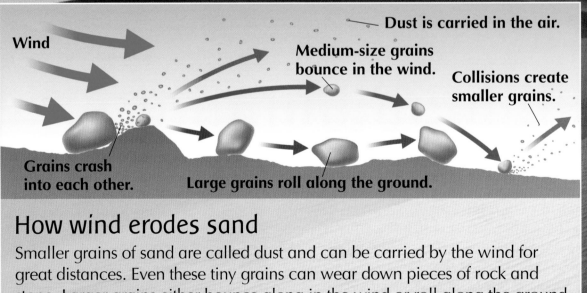

Dust is carried in the air.

Wind

Medium-size grains bounce in the wind.

Collisions create smaller grains.

Grains crash into each other.

Large grains roll along the ground.

How wind erodes sand

Smaller grains of sand are called dust and can be carried by the wind for great distances. Even these tiny grains can wear down pieces of rock and stone. Larger grains either bounce along in the wind or roll along the ground. These grains bump into each other, creating smaller and smaller grains.

Moving dunes

The hills of sand in deserts and near beaches are called dunes. These form when wind blows and deposits sand in particular places. Sand piles up on the side of a dune that faces the wind. At the crest, or top, of the mound, sand often collapses, forming a steep slope on the other side. This process also creates ripples on the dunes. Dunes can be blown away and deposited elsewhere, so that over time they appear to move.

Top Facts

- Dunes are not just sandy. Those that form at the back of some beaches are made mostly of the broken up shells of sea animals, such as mussels and clams.

- The winds that create sandstorms can blow at speeds of nearly 75 miles per hour.

Sand dunes in the desert near Dubai, United Arab Emirates

It's Amazing!

The fastest moving sand dunes on the earth were recorded in a Chinese desert in the 1950s. They moved nearly 110 yards each year for five years!

A dust storm forms in Arizona.

Dust events

The smallest grains of dust in the desert measure less than $1/250$ inch across. This dust is so light that the wind can blow it over long distances. Winds ahead of moving cold fronts (see page 159) create huge clouds of dust called dust storms. Rising warm air can send plumes of dust high into the atmosphere, where it remains, creating a dust haze.

Disappearing mountains

Mountains can disappear completely after thousands of years of weathering and erosion. Constant pounding by wind, water, and waves can leave a rock so severely eroded that there is almost nothing left!

Table Mountain sits above Cape Town, South Africa.

Mesas

Mesas are flat-topped mountains with steep cliffs around the edges, such as Table Mountain in South Africa. They are usually made of a layer of igneous rock on top of sedimentary rock. The harder rock protects the softer rock below from weathering and erosion.

Ice experiment

- Fill an empty plastic beverage bottle with water. Screw the lid on tight and place the bottle in a freezer overnight.

- Take the bottle out of the freezer the next morning. You will find that the bottle will be bulging and may have even burst open. This is because water expands, or gets bigger, when it freezes into ice.

It's Amazing!

Earthworms help to make mountains disappear! Their burrowing in mountain soil opens spaces where water and air can creep in and weather the rocks.

Scree slopes

The scree, or angular rock pieces, broken off by frost damage fall onto rock ledges and the bases of valleys. Further frost damage gradually breaks up the large scree into smaller pieces. Scree can form slopes at the base of steep cliffs or be washed farther down mountains by rain and melting snow.

From flat to hoodoo

Due to weathering, some flat areas of sedimentary rock gradually become columns called hoodoos. These columns are capped by pieces of rock that are harder than the surrounding rock. As the surrounding softer material is worn away, the rock beneath the hard stone is protected and left standing, creating a column.

Rain

Crack

Water

Ice freezes in cracks

Rock breaks off

Crack widens into wedge

Mountain hazards

Weathering can make life hazardous for mountaineers. Pieces of rock loosened by weathering may come away during a climb. Also, snow and ice may cover deep cracks in the mountain, called crevasses, which a climber could fall into.

Even on a cliff, there may be loose rocks that could prove dangerous to a climber.

Frost wedging

During cold nights, rainwater collected in cracks in rocks freezes and expands. The ice forces the crack wider. In the daytime, the ice thaws but refreezes the next night. Over time, the ice causes large pieces of rock to break off.

Wind power

The energy of the wind that wears away rocks and batters the earth during storms can also be used to power machines. Over the years, the wind has been used to grind corn, pump water, and even to create electricity.

Using wind energy

Windmills use angled blades to convert the push of wind into a rotating, or spinning, movement that can be used to power machines, such as pumps, or to spin generators to create electricity. Generators are machines with magnets and wires inside them. They convert the rotational energy of the blades into electricity. If the wind blows stronger, the blades on a windmill spin faster and the generators connected to them will create more electricity. This is why it is important to put windmills in windy places.

Windmill in Hellevoetsluis, The Netherlands

Early windmills

Windmills were widely used in Europe until the early 20th century. The windmills in The Netherlands were used to drain water from the land. This cleared land could then be used for farming.

Farm windmills

In the past, many farms in the United States used windmills to pump water up from wells deep underground. This water was then used to water crops and for animals to drink. The top of the windmill was pushed around by the wind blowing on the large triangular vane that sat behind the blades. This made sure that the windmill always faced into the wind.

Ancient windmills

Windmills with cotton sails were invented in about 200 BC—more than 2,000 years ago. Records of these machines were found in Persia, which is present-day Iran, and in China. The sails turned large, heavy stones, called millstones, that were used to grind grain into flour.

Wind farms

Wind farms are collections of tall wind turbines that generate electricity. Some of these turbines are more than 100 yards high, including the blades. Wind farms are put in places with continuous, strong winds so that they can generate a lot of power. Hilltops and coastlines are especially windy because they are places where air masses of different temperatures and pressures meet, creating wind.

A wind turbine on a wind farm on the south coast of Great Britain

It's Amazing!

Wind power provides less than 1 percent of the world's electricity. In some countries, however, wind power is more important. Nearly 10 percent of Denmark's electricity is made by wind power.

In a turbine

The turbine tower raises the blades up high, where wind speeds are greater than at ground level. The blades turn a shaft inside the box, called a nacelle, on top of the tower. The nacelle swings around to face the wind. The shaft is connected to the generator, where the rotation of the blades is turned into electricity (see opposite).

Blade

Generator

Shaft

Nacelle

Tower

Solar power

The Sun powers the water cycle, the winds, and all the weather systems on our planet. It is a plentiful source of energy that will keep burning for another four billion years. Solar technology uses the Sun's energy to heat things and to produce electricity to power machines.

Trapping heat

The simplest way to collect the sun's heat is to use a solar trap. This is a box with a glass top painted black inside to absorb the heat. Solar traps can be used as ovens to dry fruit. Other solar collectors heat water inside glass tubes. The most powerful heat collectors are solar furnaces. These use huge curved mirrors to direct heat at a box. Temperatures inside the box rise as high as 7,200 degrees Fahrenheit —enough to melt metal and even rock.

Top Facts

- Because the Sun is not visible at night, solar power systems often have batteries that store electricity for use when the Sun has set.

- We get less than 1 percent of the electricity that we use directly from solar power.

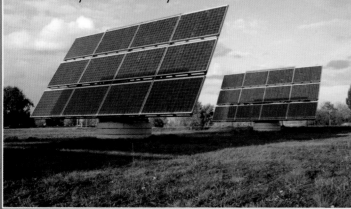

Photovoltaic arrays used to produce electricity in Germany

Solar cells

"Photovoltaic" cells, or solar cells, are thin disks of a mineral called silicon sandwiched together. When sunlight strikes the solar cells, it excites tiny particles, called electrons, and these produce an electric current. The brighter the sunlight, the greater the power produced. Cells are mounted in groups called "arrays" and are protected from the weather with a plastic covering.

Solar power stations

Some solar power stations are made up of hundreds of mirror-lined troughs that focus heat onto interconnecting pipes full of oil. The hot oil heats water, producing steam. The steam turns blades on a turbine attached to a generator that produces the electricity. The troughs tilt automatically so that they always face the Sun.

Solar-powered laptop computer

It's Amazing!

The amount of energy from the sun hitting our planet in a minute is greater than the energy that is released from burning fossil fuels over a whole year!

Small scale

Photovoltaic cells can be used to power small electronic devices, such as watches, calculators, and laptop computers. Solar power is ideal for people living in isolated, sunny places.

Huge curved mirrors used to focus sunlight at a solar furnace in Odeillo, France

Solar vehicles

Many vehicles operate using solar power. Some electric cars can run on batteries charged by solar cells. *Helios* was a solar-powered, remotely controlled airplane. Its wings were a vast curving solar panel, which produced electricity to turn the plane's many propellers. It crashed in 2003.

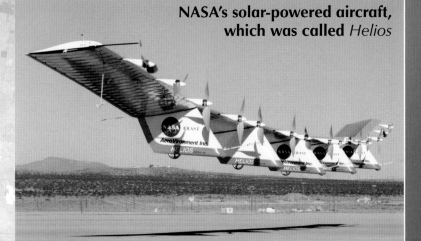

NASA's solar-powered aircraft, which was called *Helios*

Water power

The water flowing in streams and rivers has incredible force. People have been using this energy, called "hydropower," to run machines for thousands of years. More recently, giant dams have been built to convert hydropower into hydroelectricity.

The Hoover Dam is on the Arizona–Nevada border. It uses water power from the Colorado River.

Water wheel in Prague, Czech Republic

Water wheels

People first used water mills about 4,000 years ago in ancient Greece. In a mill, moving water pushed paddles on a wheel. This rotated a shaft that was connected to spinning and weaving machines to make cloth, or a millstone, which was used to grind grain.

Water pressure test

- Lie a plastic bottle on its side, and ask an adult to make one hole near the neck and one at the base. Tape over the holes, fill the bottle to the top with water and place on a tray.

- Untape both holes and see how high pressure makes the water shoot out of the lower hole much farther than water from the upper hole.

Moving water

Hydroelectric plants are built on the upper or middle courses of rivers in hills or mountains. The fast-flowing water in these upper parts of river courses is channeled past turbines that are connected to generators that make electricity. This is similar to how wind is used to produce electricity (see pages 182–183).

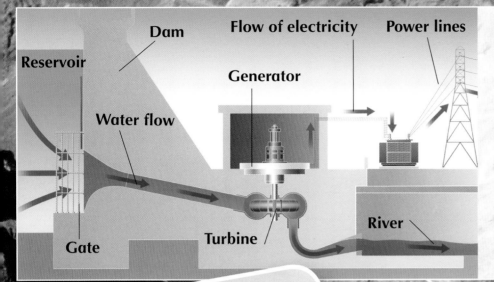

Reservoir

Dam

Flow of electricity

Power lines

Generator

Water flow

Turbine

Gate

River

Inside a dam

In a hydroelectric dam, water moves from an artificial lake, called a reservoir, past turbines to generate electricity. The electricity travels via power lines to homes. The amount of power the dam produces can be varied by closing or opening the gates from the reservoir.

It's Amazing!

Hydroelectric power stations currently provide about 20 percent of the world's electricity needs. It is easily the most used source of renewable energy.

Temple at Abu Simbel, Egypt

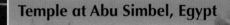

Dams

Artificial dams are huge walls that trap large amounts of river water in reservoirs. Many dams have hydroelectric turbines in pipes near their base. The deepest water is under high pressure due to the mass of water above it and it flows swiftly past the turbines. Some dams cause huge amounts of damage because their reservoirs flood land, destroying natural biomes as well as people's homes.

Abu Simbel

The ancient temples at Abu Simbel in Egypt had to be moved in the 1960s, when the Aswan Dam was built. The reservoir created by the dam flooded the temples' original site and, if the temples had not been moved, they would have been lost forever.

Wave power

Winds whip up the surface of the world's oceans into waves. Some of the wave energy that shapes coastlines and makes the ocean's surface rise and fall can be used to generate electricity. Wave power can be made on the shore or out at sea.

Making waves

When winds blow over the sea, air pushes against water, creating waves. Most wave energy is concentrated near the surface— closest to winds—and drops to almost zero by 55 yards deep. Wave height increases toward the coasts because the water is forced to pile up over the shallower sloping seabed.

Top Facts

- Little wave power is produced at present because there are not many machines in use. In the future, wave energy could produce nearly 20 percent of the power we use now.

- In 2006, a wave farm made up of Pelamis machines (see below) was built off the coast of Portugal. It can provide enough electricity to power 1,500 homes.

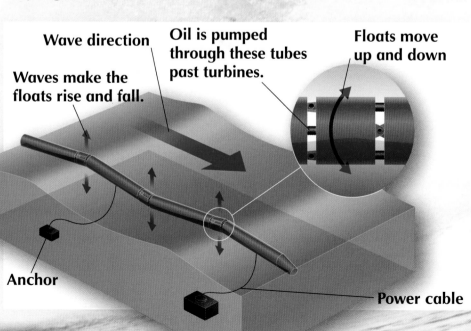

Wave direction

Waves make the floats rise and fall.

Oil is pumped through these tubes past turbines.

Floats move up and down

Anchor

Power cable

Power on the ocean

Some wave power machines float on the ocean surface, far from the coast. The "Pelamis" machine is made up of a row of floats that are anchored to the ocean floor. Waves make the floats rise and fall. This movement forces oil through tubes and past small turbines to create electricity.

Limpet wave generator in use on the coast of Scotland, Great Britain

On windy shores

Regions in the north or south temperate zones are the best places for capturing wave power because they have high winds and big waves—especially in winter. The Limpet wave generator is built into rocks on the coast of the island of Islay in Scotland, and provides the island with electricity. It was the world's first commercial wave power station.

Wave power stations

Most wave power machines use turbines to convert wave movement into rotation. This movement then turns a generator, creating electricity. Some machines use the water to spin turbines directly, but most use air or fluid pushed by the waves.

It's Amazing!

Scientists are developing a new way to deliver hydropower and water to homes at the same time. When you turn on the faucet, turbines in the pipes spin and generate power!

Inside a wave generator

In the "Limpet," rising waves enter at the base and compress, or squeeze, air trapped inside a chamber. The compressed air creates a current of air that spins the turbines. When the waves fall again, air is sucked back into the chamber, which creates more air currents that turn the turbines. The turbines are linked to generators, which turn the rotating movement into electricity.

Wave capture chamber

Turbines

Currents of air drive the turbines.

Waves compress and decompress air trapped in the chamber.

Waves enter the machine

WEATHER AND US

The weather affects our daily lives in a number of ways. It influences the food we eat, the places in which we live, and the kinds of houses we live in, as well as our health and happiness. But we also have an effect on the world's weather. Many people believe that one of the biggest challenges facing the planet today is global warming, and that this significant change in the world's climate has been caused by humans.

The weather and us

Not only does the weather play an important part in our daily lives, but it can also be important in the affairs of whole countries and cultures. The weather can play an important part in a region's wealth and industry and it can even affect international wars.

What we wear

We can control the temperature inside our buildings using heating systems and air-conditioning, but we still have to face the weather outside. In very hot places, such as the Middle East, many people wear long robes. These trap layers of air and prevent warmth from reaching the wearer's body, so they stay cool. People who live in cold places wear thick clothes, which also trap air next to the skin, but they keep the wearer warm by stopping the heat from escaping.

The Bedouin of the Sahara wear clothes that protect them from the heat.

A tropical tourist beach in the Caribbean

Weather and business

Tourism is affected by the climate because most people want hot, sunny weather when on vacation. For some countries, tourism is a major industry and bad weather or a weather disaster can be disastrous to the economy.

Farmers plow a field in Zimbabwe, Africa.

Weather and wealth

Countries with climates that suit agriculture can feed their people and sell the extra crops to make money. In places where the climate is too harsh to grow much food, people are often poor and their governments may have to import food, which is expensive. In times of drought, these countries may have to rely on food aid from charities and other nations.

It's Amazing!

The most popular tourist destination in the world is France. More than 75 million tourists visit the country each year and tourism accounts for 6 percent of the country's total income.

Weather matters

The weather can also affect our health. Hot weather increases air pollution and smog (see pages 202–203), which can cause breathing difficulties for some people. Cold weather can cause other illnesses, such as hypothermia.

A snowplow clears a runway in the United States.

Weather and travel

Weather affects almost all forms of travel. For instance, strong wind, rain, sleet, or snow can prevent planes from taking off, while snow, fallen trees, and flooding can block railroad tracks and stop trains from running. Alternatively, very hot weather can melt and crack roads and even buckle train tracks.

Weather wars

D-Day was the plan for the invasion of Europe by Allied forces during World War II. The most favorable time for the invasion was, in part, selected by weather experts. They decided that the weather during the first half of June 1944 would be the most suitable for landing troops on the beaches of Normandy, France.

People on the move

In the past, people migrated, or moved, in large numbers to find places with more favorable climates. People today still move because of the weather—they may move temporarily to flee a weather disaster or go on vacation, or they may move permanently to a warmer climate.

An Inuit hunter uses a team of dogs to pull his sled.

Past migration

The climate in different parts of the world has changed over time. In colder periods, people moved from colder areas to warmer ones, where food was easier to grow. For example, the Vikings from Scandinavia moved to land farther south, such as Great Britain. In warmer periods, food was abundant and populations increased, so people spread out and took over new places. The empire of ancient Greece, for instance, spread around the Mediterranean Sea because the warm climate brought a time of plenty.

Inuit migration

In the past, Inuit people were nomadic. They moved from place to place, following the migration routes of the animals they hunted, such as caribou, seals, and fish. These migration routes were determined by the changing weather patterns and seasons.

The seaside resort of Scarborough, Great Britain

To the seaside

In Great Britain, seaside resorts became popular during the summer in the 19th century because the climate and sea air were thought to be healthy. The building of the first railroads allowed many people to travel from the cities where they lived to the seaside for short breaks. Seaside towns, such as Scarborough, became wealthy and built grand hotels for vacationers.

Farming migration

Farmers sometimes travel with their animals to places where the weather is better. In East Africa, the farmers move their grazing animals throughout the year to places that have had recent rain to find the best areas of grass.

A family from Florida evacuate their home as Hurricane Ivan approaches in September 2004.

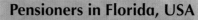
Pensioners in Florida, USA

Head for the sunshine

Many people migrate in search of better weather, especially if they are elderly. For example, between 1995 and 2000, about 149,000 more elderly people moved to the state of Florida with its warm climate, than moved away from the state.

It's Amazing!

A refugee is a person who is fleeing from a war or a natural disaster, such as a famine. In 2005, there were 8.4 million refugees around the world.

Top Facts

- More than 1 million people fled New Orleans and the surrounding area during the flooding caused by Hurricane Katrina.

- According to the International Organization for Migration, about 191 million people were classified as migrants in 2005.

Weather and health

Have you ever heard someone saying they feel "under the weather?" Weather really can affect your health. It changes your mood and affects your behavior. It can make people sick, or even kill people.

Extreme temperatures

For everything to work properly, our bodies need to stay at a constant temperature of approximately 98.6 degrees Fahrenheit. In low temperatures, our bodies stay warm by shivering. When temperatures are high, we get rid of heat by sweating. People overheat if their internal temperature rises by just 5.4 degrees Fahrenheit, or get "hypothermia," or low body heat, if it drops by just 3.6 degrees Farenheit.

Rainy days can make people feel depressed.

Moody weather

Scientists have discovered that weather really can affect your mood. They found out that people are most likely to feel depressed in cloudy weather and are happiest in dry, sunny weather that is not too hot. Most people feel better at a temperature of about 72 degrees Farenheit.

Top Facts

- **Mold grows after rain in warm seasons and releases spores into the air. Some people have an allergic reaction when they breathe in the spores.**

- **Bees can sense when a summer shower is on the way, so they stay close to their hive because they could be injured by the rain.**

Bees on a honeycomb

Ideal conditions

Humidity levels can also affect people's alertness and activity as well as their mood. For example, school children fidget, make more mistakes, and cannot concentrate on warm and humid days. Their mood often improves after it rains. This is because the rain helps to cool the air, which reduces any feelings of tiredness and lethargy.

A rain shower on a very hot day can reduce the temperature and improve a person's mood.

It's Amazing!
In Finland, the mortality rate increases by 0.2 percent for every degree the temperature drops below 64 degrees Fahrenheit.

Feel the heat

Hot summers cause some people to behave irrationally. New York City, for example, experiences regular summer crime waves, which are believed to be a result of the hot weather. Hot, humid days are the worst for bad behavior.

Ill winds

Some winds are known as "ill winds" because they are linked to stress, depression, and sleepless nights. The Mistral is a cold wind that blows across France. The wind's strength, which blows for more than 100 days a year, is said to give people headaches and even drive some people mad.

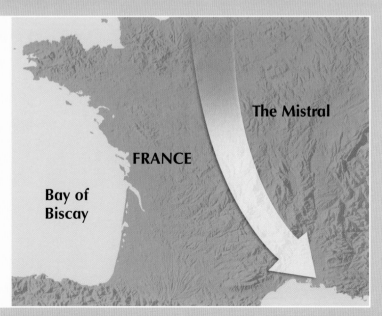
The Mistral

FRANCE

Bay of Biscay

Farming

A region's climate will affect what plants can grow there. This, in turn, will have an affect on what people living in the region are able to grow on farms and, ultimately, what they can eat.

Planning for the weather

Farmers have to consider the weather at all times. It affects what crops they grow and when they can plant and harvest them. No amount of careful planning, however, can save a farmer's crops from drought, flood, hail, frosts, or any of the pests or diseases that can thrive in certain weather conditions.

Rice Paddy in Burma

Rice fields

Rice is an important food for over half the people in the world. Rice only grows in wet, tropical areas. It is the only cereal crop that needs to grow with its roots under water. In many places, people wait for the monsoon floods before planting rice seedlings in flooded fields, called paddies.

A plastic greenhouse for lettuce in France

Make your own weather

Greenhouses create artificial weather conditions to allow farmers to produce crops that would not normally grow in the local climate. These glass or plastic structures trap the sun's heat, keeping the air inside warm and sheltering plants from the wind.

It's Amazing!

Half a billion people in Africa and Asia eat a type of banana called a plantain as a major part of their diet. The plant will only grow in warm, tropical climates.

Rain on demand

People can make storm clouds drop rain on demand. To do this, an airplane flies above a storm cloud and drops particles of a chemical, such as silver iodide, into it. This causes water droplets to gather around the particles. The droplets turn into snow and eventually fall as rain. This process is called "seeding," and is sometimes used over places that are experiencing drought.

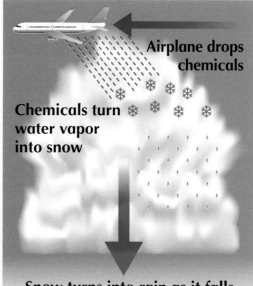

Airplane drops chemicals

Chemicals turn water vapor into snow

Snow turns into rain as it falls.

Cranberry harvest in Wisconsin. Cranberries need a lot of water to grow. The fields are flooded to make the fruit easier to harvest and to protect it from frost.

Growing fruit

Some fruit grows only in tropical climates with hot, humid conditions all year round. Tropical fruit includes bananas, pineapples, and mangoes. Citrus fruit, such as oranges and lemons, grows in Mediterranean climates, which are warm and dry most of the year. In cooler regions, people have to import citrus and tropical fruits, or grow them in greenhouses. Some countries often import fruit they cannot produce themselves, such as American cranberries, which grow only in certain parts of the United States.

Top Facts

- In the United States, cloud seeding is carried out over areas having a drought and to clear fog from airports. Sometimes it is used at ski resorts to encourage more snow to fall.

- Climate patterns mean that nearly 38 percent of all land on the Earth is used for farming.

Houses and homes

Weather and climate greatly influence where people build their homes and the type of houses they choose to live in. In the past, few people lived in deserts, but today buildings can be designed to cope with many extremes of temperature and weather.

Hot houses

Buildings often have many features to make them more comfortable for their occupants. For example, many homes built in hot countries are painted white to reflect heat. They may also have slatted windows made from strips of wood. These windows let air through but block out some sunlight, which helps to keep the inside cool. In Pakistan, many houses have wind catchers on their roofs. These trap passing drafts of wind and direct them down into the house to provide a cooling breeze.

Hard roofs

In places where there is heavy snow in winter, such as Switzerland, many buildings have a strong roof built at a steep angle. The sloping roof helps the snow to slide off. If the snow settled and built up, its weight could make the roof collapse.

A wooden chalet in France

An underground home in Coober Pedy, Australia

Underground living

Some people in the town of Coober Pedy, which is located in the desert in the middle of Australia, have dug their houses underground to escape the heat. These homes are pleasantly cool, but electricity is essential because they do not have any natural light.

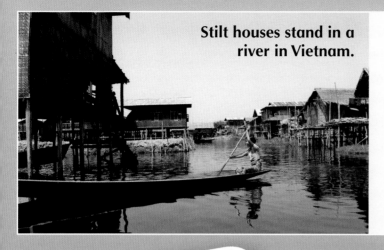

Stilt houses stand in a river in Vietnam.

High and dry

In some parts of the world, people cannot afford to move away from areas where floods happen frequently, so they build their homes up high to avoid the water. These houses in Vietnam are raised above the ground on wooden stilts. In times of flooding, people travel between the houses by boat.

Snow homes

Inuit people living in the Arctic Circle sometimes build igloos. Blocks of snow are made into a circular base and then more blocks are added, making a dome-shaped structure with an entrance tunnel on one side. Snow is such a good insulator that it keeps the inside of the igloo warm even though the outside walls are frozen.

It's Amazing!

Some houses in Holland can float. They are made of lightweight materials that allow them to float if it floods!

The igloo provides shelter and warmth, despite being built from blocks of ice.

Passive houses

"Passive houses" were invented in 1988. They need very little energy to heat them and are popular in parts of northern Europe. Each house has thick walls and triple-glazed windows to trap heat inside. The house is heated mostly by sunlight and the heat given off by light bulbs and refrigerators.

Smog

Smog is a kind of thick, dirty fog. It often forms over cities on warm summer days. From a distance, smog looks like a giant brown cloud, and it can cover a large area, greatly reducing both visibility and air quality.

Air pollution

Smog forms because of pollution in the air. There are two main types of smog, sulfurous smog and photochemical smog. Sulfurous smog is largely caused by burning fossil fuels such as coal. The main polluting gas in photochemical smog is ozone—a type of oxygen that is created in the air from smoke and the fumes, or gases, released by motor vehicles. The layer of ozone gas high up in the atmosphere protects us from many of the sun's harmful rays. At ground level, however, ozone can be harmful.

London smogs

In 1952, thousands of people in London died when smoke from factories and houses made smog that was deadly. Lethal smogs like these stopped in Great Britain after the Clean Air Act of 1956, which allowed people to use only smokeless fuels in certain areas.

People wear masks to protect them from smog in Linfen, China.

Sunlight

Polluting gases trapped by layer of warm air

Pollution

Factory smoke

Vehicle fumes

Smog

Methane from trees

Photochemical smog

When polluting gases react with sunlight, they create photochemical smog. These gases include vehicle fumes and natural gases, such as methane. When a layer of warm air passes over an area, these polluting gases are trapped near the ground, forming the smog.

Polluting gas

Before cars, most smog was caused by smoke from coal fires. Today, about 95 percent of the gases that cause smog are made when fossil fuels, such as gasoline and oil, are used to power factories and vehicles or burned in power stations to make electricity.

A cloud of polluting smoke hangs above a cement factory.

Smog hazards

Smog affects people's health and can cause headaches, dizziness, and breathing problems. It particularly affects the elderly, the very young and people who have heart disease or asthma. In cities with severe smog, people wear masks over their mouths and noses to reduce the amount of polluted air they breathe in.

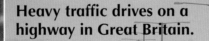

Heavy traffic drives on a highway in Great Britain.

Exhaust fumes

On busy streets, slow-moving cars produce a lot of fumes. Today, many cars are fitted with "catalytic converters," devices that reduce the amount of harmful gases they produce. These devices do not, however, stop all fumes, and with increasing numbers of cars on the roads, pollution levels remain very high.

Acid rain

Acid rain is precipitation that has been polluted by gases in the atmosphere. It is caused by smoke and fumes from factories and motor vehicles. When acid rain falls from the sky, it can damage trees and plants, pollute lakes, erode stone buildings, and even kill animals.

How acid rain forms

Factories, power stations, and vehicles release the gases sulfur dioxide and nitrogen oxide into the air. When these polluting gases react with water vapor in the air, they form particles of sulfuric acid and nitric acid, which fall to the ground in rain or snow.

Damage to a pine tree in the Czech Republic caused by acid rain

The acid test

- Put some carbonated cola beverage in a dish or jar and drop in a dirty coin.
- After a few hours, rinse the coin. It will be clean and shiny because the acid in the beverage has dissolved the dirt.
- You can try this with a baby tooth that has fallen out. After a few days, the tooth will disappear completely because it will have been eaten away by the beverage!

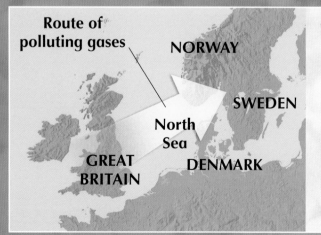

Route of polluting gases

NORWAY

SWEDEN

North Sea

GREAT BRITAIN

DENMARK

Where acid rain happens

Acid rain may fall near the factories or vehicles that produce the pollution, but winds in the troposphere can carry the gases far from their source. For example, sulfur dioxide from coal-burning power stations in Great Britain has been carried to Scandinavia, where it pollutes lakes, kills fish, and damages plant life.

Fish killed by pollution caused by acid rain

What acid rain does

The acids in acid rain are powerful chemicals that can even dissolve metal. These airborne acids are bad for the lungs if people breathe them in. They also erode objects made from metal and certain stones, such as marble and limestone. In some parts of the world, acid rain has damaged historic statues and buildings—including the Taj Mahal, a large, ornate tomb in India.

It's Amazing!

In Sweden, acid rain has made more than 18,000 lakes so acidic that all the fish and other creatures that lived in them have died. This acid rain has been caused by polluting gases released all over Europe.

Dead wildlife

Some acid rain runs off the land and drains into lakes and rivers. Acid lake water makes the soil on the lake bed release the metal aluminum. This metal is poisonous to many plants, fish and insects—and can kill them.

Damage to a Swedish forest caused by acid rain

Failing forests

Acid rain damages and kills trees in two ways. First, the acid damages the tree's leaves, which affects its ability to make food by photosynthesis (see page 70). Then, when acid rain soaks into the ground and builds up there, it reduces the nutrients in the soil that trees absorb through their roots and need to survive.

The ozone layer

High in the atmosphere, approximately 15 miles above the ground, is a layer that contains a lot of ozone (see page 202). This ozone layer absorbs harmful UV rays in sunlight. However, it is slowly being destroyed by pollution in the atmosphere.

Ozone holes

Scientists first discovered a hole in the ozone layer in the 1970s when they were studying the atmosphere over Antarctica. Since that time, images taken by satellites have shown that there are ozone holes over other parts of the world, including Europe. In fact, the holes are not really gaps but areas where there is a much lower amount of ozone gas than normal. This reduction in ozone gas means that the ozone layer is not as good at protecting the earth from harmful UV rays.

Always wear plenty of sunscreen on the beach.

More UV rays

UV rays can cause skin cancer and eye damage in people and other animals, and reduce the growth rate of some plants. Everyone should wear sunglasses and sunscreen, and cover up in the sunshine to avoid being harmed by UV rays.

Refrigerator pile

Many countries have banned the use of ozone-depleting gases. In some places, thousands of old refrigerators have been dumped while experts try to find a way of disposing of them without releasing the ozone-depleting gases they contain.

A pile of refrigerators in Great Britain

It's Amazing!

The ozone hole over Antarctica covers a greater area than the whole of North America.

What causes ozone holes?

When certain gases are released into the atmosphere, they react with ozone and deplete, or destroy, it. The main ozone-depleting gases are called CFCs (chlorofluorocarbons). These are found in aerosols, refrigerators and car air-conditioning systems. Other ozone-depleting gases are halons, which are used in fire extinguishers, and nitrous oxides, used in some fertilizers.

South America

A satellite image of the southern hemisphere shows the size of the ozone hole on September 17, 2001.

The ozone hole

Antarctica

A growing problem?

The hole in the ozone layer over Antarctica grew in size until, by 2000, it covered 11 million square miles. In recent years, scientists reported that the hole seemed to have stopped growing. It is hoped that it may fully recover within the next 60 years.

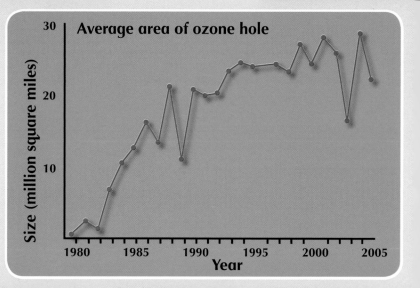

Average area of ozone hole

Size (million square miles)

Year

What is global warming?

Global warming is the rise in the temperature of Earth's atmosphere, which causes changes in the world's climate. Global temperatures have risen in the past 140 years at a much faster rate than at any other time in the past 1,000 years.

Climate change

Throughout the history of Earth, the planet's climate has varied. These natural changes have taken place over long periods of time and have led to events, such as ice ages (see page 59). Scientists believe that, in about 50 years, the rise in world temperatures will start to have a great effect on Earth.

It's Amazing!
Scientists predict that Earth's temperature could rise by up to 12 degrees Farenheit by the year 2100.

A iceberg melts in the Southern Ocean near Antarctica.

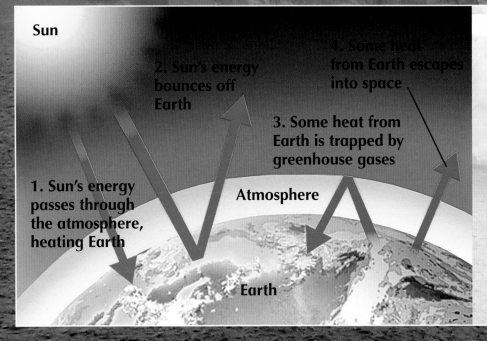

Sun

2. Sun's energy bounces off Earth

4. Some heat from Earth escapes into space

3. Some heat from Earth is trapped by greenhouse gases

1. Sun's energy passes through the atmosphere, heating Earth

Atmosphere

Earth

Greenhouse effect

The Sun's rays heat Earth (1). Some of this heat escapes back into space (2 and 4). However, some of the heat is trapped in the atmosphere by greenhouse gases (3). These gases include carbon dioxide, and they act like a blanket, warming up the earth. This warming effect is called the greenhouse effect because the gases act similar to the glass in a greenhouse.

Where is affected?

The coldest, most remote places on Earth, such as parts of Alaska, Canada, Siberia, the Arctic, and Antarctica, have already warmed up much more than other places. As a result, large areas of ice and permafrost (see page 49) are melting. The plants, animals, and people that live in these places are already being affected by global warming, but eventually the effects will be felt all over the world.

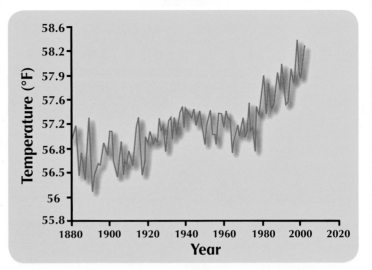

Rising temperatures

This graph shows that the global average temperature has risen by nearly 0.5 degrees Fahrenheit between 1880 and today. In recent times, temperatures have been getting even warmer—the four warmest years of the 20th century all happened in the 1990s.

A scientist checks on an ice sample taken from Greenland.

Looking at global warming

Scientists can study global warming by taking samples of ice from below the surface near the poles. This deep ice is thousands of years old and contains tiny bubbles of air. Scientists study these air bubbles, recording the levels of certain gases inside them. These gases tell the scientists what the climate was like thousands of years ago and, therefore, how much warmer it is today.

Top Facts

- The Arctic has always been covered in ice, but within 60 years or so this ice could melt every summer.

- White ice reflects heat. As the ice caps melt, the darker color of the land or ocean is revealed. These darker colors absorb heat, and further speed up the melting of the ice.

Causes of global warming

Many scientists believe that human activity is causing global warming. They say that the rate of change has speeded up greatly since the late 18th century, when people began to use fossil fuels, such as oil, coal, and gas, to make electricity and other forms of energy.

Pumping fumes

Gases that contain high levels of carbon add to the greenhouse effect (see page 208) and global warming. These gases include carbon dioxide and methane. When we burn fossil fuels in vehicles and in power stations and factories, we release carbon dioxide back into the air and upset the delicate balance of gases in the atmosphere.

It's Amazing!

In a single day, one cow can release 8½ ounces of methane into the air. There are about 1.5 billion cows on Earth, so that is a lot of methane!

Methane

Methane traps about 20 times more heat than carbon dioxide. Methane forms when plants rot and it is released into the air from coal mines, oil and gas wells, rice paddies, and landfill sites filled with household garbage. Bacteria in a cow's stomach convert some food into methane, which is released when cows belch and release gas!

Who pollutes?

In general, wealthy countries produce more greenhouse gases than poor countries. For example, the United States is the world's leading producer of carbon dioxide gas. However, some poorer countries are increasing the amount of carbon dioxide they produce as their industries grow. In recent years, for instance, China has overtaken Europe as the second largest producer of carbon dioxide after the United States.

Large, off-road cars driven in wealthy countries produce a lot of carbon dioxide.

Forest fuel

When rainforests are burned to clear land for farming or building, the carbon dioxide stored in the plants is released into the atmosphere. Growing trees absorb carbon dioxide, so by cutting down rainforests we are reducing the amount of carbon dioxide absorbed from the atmosphere.

Hot-house theory

Swedish chemist Svante Arrhenius developed the theory of global warming in the early 1890s. He worked out that if the carbon dioxide released by coal-burning industries doubled, world temperatures could increase by 7 to 11 degrees Fahrenheit. His "hot-house theory" has only recently been widely accepted.

A satellite image shows areas of cleared rainforest (light red) next to areas of intact forest (dark red) in Rondonia, Brazil.

Farming and fertilizers

As the world's population increases, many farmers are using chemical fertilizers to increase the amount of crops produced each year. Fertilizers give off the greenhouse gas nitrous oxide when they are made in factories and sprayed on fields. Farm machinery that runs on fossil fuels also adds to global warming.

A German farmer sprays his field with chemical fertilizer.

A warmer planet

Many climate experts predict that the average temperature on Earth will continue to increase in the next 100 years. They prefer the term "climate change" to "global warming" because an increase in world temperatures would have many different effects.

Top Facts

- Global sea levels could rise by almost 3 feet by 2100.
- Climate change could alter one-third of all plant and animal habitats by the end of the 21st century.

Rising sea levels

Climate change will have a variety of effects. Regions with wet, snowy climates may get hotter and drier. Lakes and rivers may dry up, and there could be water shortages in some places. Sea levels will rise as the ice around the poles melts and ocean waters warm and expand. A rise in sea levels of just 3 feet would flood 6 percent of The Netherlands.

A palm tree grows on the Marshall Islands in the Pacific Ocean. If sea levels continue to rise, then these islands will be submerged.

The human impact

Climate change will increase the number of droughts and make it harder to grow crops in some areas. There is also likely to be an increase in insect pests that thrive in warmer climates. Some insects, such as mosquitoes, spread disease. Large quantities of pesticides may need to be sprayed to kill off these insects.

Spraying for mosquitoes in Sri Lanka

Wildlife

Some animals may become extinct as the climate changes. Many of the species at risk live on low-lying land near the sea or at the poles. Polar bears hunt seals on floating sea ice. As the ice disappears, so might the polar bears.

A polar bear hunts on sea ice near Greenland.

Extreme weather

Global warming increases the risk of extreme weather. Hurricanes form over warm ocean waters, and tornadoes form over warm land, so global warming will bring an increase in both. Warmer oceans will also mean more water evaporates. This will lead to heavier monsoon rains and more floods as clouds release the extra water over land. Heat waves may happen more often, and, as forests get hotter and drier, there is also an increased risk of wildfires.

It's Amazing!

Scientists have worked out that global sea levels have already risen by 10 inches over the last 100 years—and they are continuing to rise!

Coral reef found in the Red Sea off the coast of Egypt

Coral reefs

Coral reefs are home to one fourth of all the marine animals in the world. They also shelter coastal areas from storms. Coral reefs are built by colonies of tiny animals called coral polyps. As water temperatures rise, many reefs lose the algae that live inside the polyps. Without the algae, the polyps may die and the reefs may disappear.

The future of our climate

In 2007, United Nations scientists warned that, to avoid climate change, carbon dioxide levels must not rise and should be reduced by about one-third by 2100. So, what are the solutions to climate change for the future?

Kyoto treaty

The United Nations holds meetings where world leaders agree on what to do about climate change. In 1997, the Kyoto treaty was first negotiated. Many countries signed up to this treaty and have agreed to cut the amount of carbon dioxide and other greenhouse gases released into the atmosphere.

A cyclist uses a cycle lane in The Netherlands.

Individual action

Everyone can help reduce climate change. You can save fuel by cycling to school, using public transportation or by sharing a car. You can save energy by switching off televisions and lights when they are not needed. Recycling glass, paper and cans and reusing plastic bags and envelopes also helps.

It's Amazing!

There are some incredible ideas about how to solve climate change. One of the strangest is to put a giant cloud of moon dust above the earth to block out sunlight!

The United Nations logo

Renewable energy

One way to reduce the amount of carbon dioxide released into the atmosphere is to use renewable energy. In some countries, governments are investing more money in renewable energy projects, such as wind and water power. Many individuals are installing solar panels in their homes to heat water and make electricity.

A solar panel uses sunlight to make electricity.

Predictions

Carbon dioxide stays in the atmosphere for 100 years, so we cannot easily undo the damage already done. The best solution seems to be to reduce greenhouse gases to ensure global warming is gradual. This would give living things time to adapt to climate change.

Your eco footprint

- Your ecological footprint is a measure of how much land and water you need to 'offset' or balance what you use and what you throw away. It is a way of finding out how environmentally friendly you and your family are.

- All you have to do is answer the questions at www.earthday.net/footprint.

Global action

Many people believe that governments should take more action. World leaders could, for example, allow only coal power stations that trap and store any carbon dioxide released, or they could encourage people to use alternatives to gasoline, such as biofuels made from certain crops.

Canola is used to make low-polluting biofuel.

GLOSSARY

Aerial
Describes something that is carried by the air or flies through it.

Air
The gases that make up the atmosphere.

Air pressure
The weight of the air pushing down on Earth's surface.

Anemometer
A device used to measure the force or speed of wind.

Antarctica
The region around the South Pole.

Anticyclone
A system of winds that spins in a clockwise direction in the Northern Hemisphere, and counterclockwise in the Southern Hemisphere.

Arctic
The region around the North Pole.

Atmosphere
A layer of gas around a planet. Earth's atmosphere is over 300 miles thick.

Aurorae
Colorful displays of lights high in Earth's atmosphere. They are caused by charged particles from the Sun reacting with gases in the atmosphere.

Axis
An imaginary line around which an object rotates. Earth's axis runs through the North Pole and the South Pole.

Barometer
A device that is used to measure air pressure.

Biome
A type of natural environment that covers a large area, such as a desert, a wetland, a grassland, or a rainforest.

Carbon dioxide
A clear gas that has no smell. It is breathed out by animals and humans, while plants use it to make sugars. Carbon dioxide is believed to be a major cause of the greenhouse effect and may be responsible for changing the planet's climate.

Charged particles
These are particles that have an electric charge. These particles can have either a positive or a negative charge.

Chlorophyll
The green chemical that is found in the leaves of plants and is used to turn sunlight, water, and carbon dioxide into sugars, which the plants then use to grow. This process is called photosynthesis.

Climate
The pattern of weather in an area. All plants and animals are suited to live in their native climate.

Climograph
A graph showing the climate in a region throughout the year. It usually records the changes in temperature and rainfall.

Condense
Of a gas—to cool and contract to form a liquid. For example, the gas water vapor condenses to form droplets of liquid water.

Continent
One of Earth's seven large land areas, which are Asia, Australasia, Europe, North America, South America, and Antarctica.

Contract
To get smaller.

Cyclone
A system of winds that rotates, or spins, in a counterclockwise direction in the Northern Hemisphere, and clockwise in the Southern Hemisphere.

Delta
Where a river meets the sea. The river drops stones and mud to create a triangular system of small river channels that make up the delta.

Density
The amount of mass a substance has for each unit of volume.

Depression
An area of low air pressure.

Desert
An area of land that receives little or no rain during the year. As life needs water to survive, fewer plants and animals live in deserts than in other biomes.

Dew point
The temperature at which water vapor condenses to form water droplets in the air.

Equator
The imaginary line that runs around Earth halfway between the two poles.

Evaporate
To change from a liquid into a gas, for instance when liquid water turns into the gas water vapor.

Expand
To get bigger.

Fossil
Evidence of a dead animal or plant, which has been preserved in rock or another substance, such as amber. Fossils are usually millions of years old.

Front
The edge of an air mass. Weather fronts usually bring a change in weather as they pass over.

Germination
When a plant starts to grow.

Gravity
The force of attraction between any two objects, such as the pull between the Earth and the Moon.

Greenhouse effect
The warming of the climate due to the presence of greenhouse gases, such as carbon dioxide, in the atmosphere. These stop heat escaping from the atmosphere. Pollution is causing an increase in the greenhouse effect, and the world is heating up.

Habitat
The place where an animal or plant lives.

Heat wave
A period with high temperatures.

Hemisphere
One half of Earth. The Northern Hemisphere lies north of the equator and the Southern Hemisphere lies south of it.

Herd
A large group of hoofed mammals that live together.

Hibernation
A deep sleep that some animals go into to survive the winter. Their heart rate slows down and the animals appear to be dead.

Humidity
The amount of water vapor that is in the air.

Hurricane
A large, spinning tropical storm that forms in the western Atlantic Ocean and has powerful winds that blow at more than 75 miles per hour.

Hydroelectric power
Electricity created by the movement of water. Water flows over a turbine causing it to spin. The turbine is connected to a generator and the spinning motion creates electricity.

Hygrometer
A device used to measure the humidity of air.

Ice caps
The thick layers of ice and snow that cover the North and South Poles.

Infrared radiation
A form of light energy. It is invisible to the human eye, but it can be detected as a warm feeling on the skin.

Irrigate

To water a crop, either by spraying water directly onto the plants or by digging channels that carry water to the plants from another water source, such as a lake.

Longshore drift

The movement of sand and stones along a beach. These particles of sand and stone are pushed along the beach by waves hitting the shore at a slight angle.

Magma

The molten, or liquid, rock under the surface of Earth that rises up through volcanoes.

Migration

The movement of animals or people from one region to another.

Monsoon

A seasonal wind that blows in one direction for six months and then reverses its direction for the other six months. The Indian monsoon blows from the land to the sea during the winter months. In summer, it blows in the opposite direction, bringing heavy, cooling rains off the Indian Ocean.

Moraines

Collections of rocks, stones, and clay left behind by a glacier.

Orbit

The path of one body in space around another. For example, Earth orbits the Sun and weather satellites orbit Earth.

Photosynthesis

The process plants use to turn energy from sunlight, carbon dioxide, and water into sugars, which they use to grow. This forms the basis for all other life as it is the only way in nature to take energy from sunlight.

Psychrometer

A type of hygrometer that consists of two thermometers, one wet and one dry. It is used to measure the humidity of air.

Radar

A device that uses pulses of radio waves to detect objects, including rain storms. The device sends out invisible radio waves and these bounce off the storms back to the device as echoes. By listening to these echoes, the device can build up a picture of where the storms are and even how strong they are.

Radiosonde

A small radio device that is carried into the air, usually by a weather balloon. It sends back information about weather conditions high in the atmosphere.

Rainforest

A dense kind of forest found in areas with high rainfall. They are usually found near to the equator.

Rain gauge

A device that records the amount of rain that has fallen on that spot.

Rain seeding

Adding chemicals to clouds to encourage the formation of rain. These chemicals can be dropped from planes or shot up in rockets.

Renewable energy

A source of energy, such as wind power or solar power, which cannot be used up.

Reservoir

An artificial lake that is built to store water. This water can either be used for drinking or it can be chaneled through turbines that are connected to generators to produce electricity.

Right angle

When one object or path is at 90 degrees to another.

Satellite

Any object that orbits a planet. A satellite is held in orbit by the planet's gravity.

Seasons

Periods with their own weather patterns. For example, summer is a season that usually has dry, warm weather, while winter is a season that has cold weather.

Sediment

Small pieces of rock or soil that settle at the bottom of rivers and oceans and on beaches.

Static electricity

An electrical charge that is produced by rubbing an object.

Temperate zones

Regions that lie in the Northern and Southern Hemispheres between the tropical zones and the polar zones. They usually have warm summer seasons and cold winter seasons.

Tornado

A narrow column of violently spinning air. The powerful winds in a tornado blow at speeds of about 300 miles per hour.

Trade wind

The name given to a wind that blows constantly in one direction. Hundreds of years ago, these winds were used to blow ships carrying goods over the oceans to trade in other countries.

Tropical storm

A storm that forms in the tropical zone and may grow in strength to become a hurricane.

Tropical zone

The region that lies on either side of the equator.

Tundra

A cold, treeless region next to the polar zones where the soil below the surface is frozen all year round. This frozen layer is called permafrost and its presence prevents the growth of large plants such as trees.

Turbine

A set of angled blades that spins around when water or air flows over it. Turbines are attached to generators, which turn the spinning motion of the blades into electricity.

Ultraviolet radiation

A form of light energy that cannot be seen with the human eye.

United Nations

An international organization that was set up in 1945 after World War II. Among its many roles, it creates and enforces international agreements, such as the Kyoto treaty, which is an international agreement on climate change.

Water cycle

The movement of water from one form to another in the atmosphere. For example, rain falls onto the ground, it collects into streams and rivers, and these flow into lakes and seas. Here the water evaporates to form water vapor, which later condenses to form water droplets to create clouds. These water droplets then fall as rain, starting the cycle again.

Water vapor

Water in the form of a gas. Water vapor forms when liquid water in lakes and seas evaporates. Water vapor then condenses to form water droplets that make up clouds.

Whiteout

A condition that forms when a blizzard is so bad that few objects are visible and the horizon cannot be seen.

Wind chill

The cooling effect created by a wind.

INDEX

ACKNOWLEDGMENTS

Artwork supplied through the Art Agency by Peter Bull

Photo credits:
b = bottom, t = top, r = right, l = left, c = center

Front cover c Momatiuk - Eastcott/Corbis, tl Robert Glusic/Corbis, tc Ralph A. Clevenger/CORBIS, tr Paul Freytag/zefa/Corbis, bl Warren Faidley/Corbis, br Arthur Morris/CORBIS
Back cover bl Gerolf Kalt/zefa/Corbis, tl Maxfx/Dreamstime.com, tr Frans Lanting/Corbis, bc Gerolf Kalt/zefa/Corbis

1 Paul A. Souders/Corbis, 2-3 NASA, 4-5 Maxfx/Dreamstime.com, 8-9 Gianni Giansanti/Corbis, 10 bl Chrisdodutch/Dreamstime.com, 11b Dreamstime.com, 12–13 Paul A. Souders/Corbis, 12b NASA, 13t NASA, 13b Dreamstime.com, 15t Sebastian/Dreamstime.com, 15cr Dreamstime.com/Carolyne Pehora, 16-17 NASA, 17t Dreamstime.com/Joe Gough, 16-17b Mike Nettleship/Dreamstime.com, 18-19 Dreamstime.com/Jeff Waibel, 18b Slawomir Jastrzebski/Dreamstime.com, 19t Igor Kharlamov/Dreamstime.com, 19b Dreamstime.com, 21t Andrew Kazmierski/Dreamstime.com, 21b Digital Vision, 22–23 Craig Tuttle/Corbis, 22b iStockphoto.com, 23t Annie Griffiths Belt/Corbis, 23b Gennadij Kurilin/Dreamstime.com, 24 Dreamstime.com/Nicky Linzey, 24b Kevin Fleming/Corbis, 25 Joe Gough/Dreamstime.com, 25t Jason Maehl/Dreamstime.com, 25b Scott Collis/Dreamstime.com, 26-27 Dreamstime.com/Mike Carlson and Heike Mirabella/Dreamstime.com, 26t Don Mace/Dreamstime.com, 27t Dreamstime.com, 27b Dreamstime.com/Will Moneymaker, 28-29 Neil Rabinowitz/Corbis, 28cl Adam Booth/Dreamstime.com, 29cl Joe Gough/Dreamstime.com, 29br Harris Shiffman/Dreamstime.com, 30cl NASA, 30br Martin Brown/Dreamstime.com, 31tr Museum of the City of New York/Corbis, 32-33 Danny Lehman/Corbis, 32tr Dreamstime.com/Steve Lovegrove, 33b Dreamstime.com/Luke Pederson, 34-35 John Conrad/Corbis, 36-37 Nick Stubbs/Dreamstime.com, 36t Christine Schneider/zefa/Corbis, 37cr Dreamstime.com, 38 Dreamstime.com/Vladimir Pomortsev, 38b Charles O'Rear/Corbis, 39 Dreamstime.com/Pete Favelle, 40-41 Sharna Balfour; Gallo Images/Corbis, 41bl Keren Su/Corbis, 42b Peter Elvidge/Dreamstime.com, 43cr Digital Vision, 44-45 Frans Lanting/Corbis, 44b Dreamstime.com/Matthias Weinrich, 45t Dreamstime.com, 45bl Gavin Bates/Dreamstime.com, 45br Marbo/Dreamstime.com, 46-47 Dreamstime.com/Anthony Hathaway, 47cl Dreamstime.com/Bernard Breton, 48-49 Richard Hamilton Smith/Corbis, 48bl Dreamstime.com/Dcrippen, 48br Gail Johnson/Dreamstime.com, 50-51 Günter Rossenbach/zefa/Corbis, 50b David Lloyd/Dreamstime.com, 51t James Hearn/Dreamstime.com, 52 Dreamstime.com/Martina Berg, 53bl Jean-marc Strydom/Dreamstime.com, 53br Sean Nel/Dreamstime.com, 54-55 Frank Lane Picture Agency/Corbis, 54bl Steve Mcwilliam/Dreamstime.com, 55cr Ismael Montero/Dreamstime.com, 56-57 Richard T. Nowitz/Corbis, 56tr Dreamstime.com, 58-59 Gary Braasch/Corbis, 59br Kris Hanke/Dreamstime.com, 60-61 Franz-Marc Frei/Corbis, 62-63 Gerolf Kalt/zefa/Corbis, 62bl www.novacelestia.com, 63t Jhaviv/Dreamstime.com, 63b Dreamstime.com, 64-65 Theo Allofs/zefa/Corbis, 65b Tim Wimbourne/Reuters/Corbis, 66-67 Cecilia Enholm/Etsa/Corbis, 66t Dreamstime.com, 67br George McCarthy/Corbis, 68-69 Niall Benvie/Corbis, 68tl Dreamstime.com/Jens Mayer, 69tr Tom Davison/Dreamstime.com, 69br Clouds Hill Imaging Ltd./Corbis, 70-71 Bob Krist/Corbis, 71tl courtesy of John Deere, 71br Dreamstime.com, 72-73 Bob Krist/Corbis, 72t Dreamstime.com, 72b Christophe D./Dreamstime.com, 74-75 Will & Deni McIntyre/Corbis, 74t Dreamstime.com/Edite Artmann, 75tr Niall Benvie/Corbis, 75bl Dreamstime.com/Anna Kowalska, 75bc Lauren Jones/Dreamstime.com, 75br Dreamstime.com/Jason Cheever, 76-77 Peggy Heard; Frank Lane Picture Agency/Corbis, 76bl Vadim Kozlovsky/Dreamstime.com, 77tr Dreamstime.com, 77br Dreamstime.com/Aaron Whitney, 78 Heng Sinith/epa/Corbis, 78tl Digital Vision, 78br Dreamstime.com, 79 Michael S. Yamashita/Corbis, 80-81 Rob Howard/Corbis, 81cr Shawna Caldwell/Dreamstime.com, 82-83 Frans Lanting/Corbis, 82b Colleen Coombe/Dreamstime.com, 83t Jim Parkin/Dreamstime.com, 84-85 Max Blain/Dreamstime.com, 84tr Thomas Perkins/Dreamstime.com, 85tr Tall Tree Ltd, 85br Dreamstime.com/Zinchik, 86-87 Eric Nguyen/Corbis, 88-89 Jim Reed/Corbis, 88b Graham Prentice/Dreamstime.com, 89tr Ray Bird; Frank Lane Picture Agency/Corbis, 89b NASA, 90-91 Jon Hicks/Corbis, 91t Reuters/Corbis, 91b Imre Forgo/Dreamstime.com, 92-93 Luca Zennaro/epa/Corbis, 92tl Reuters/Corbis, 92b Dreamstime.com, 93t Dreamstime.com, 94-95 Lynsey Addario/Corbis, 94b Neil Wigmore/Dreamstime.com, 95tr Gideon Mendel/Corbis, 95bl Dreamstime.com, 96-97 Paul Thompson; Ecoscene/Corbis, 97t Wolfgang Kumm/epa/Corbis, 97bl Florea Marius Catalin/Dreamstime.com, 98-99 Barry Lewis/Corbis, 98tl John Noble/Corbis, 98 Digital Vision, 99cr William Attard Mccarthy/Dreamstime.com, 100-101 Layne Kennedy/Corbis, 101cl Buffalo News/Mike Groll/Corbis Sygma, 101bl Annie Griffiths Belt/Corbis, 102-103 NASA, 102tl Dreamstime.com/Greg Pelt, 103b Dreamstime.com, 104-105 Aaron Horowitz/Corbis, 105t Bettmann/Corbis, 105b Dreamstime.com, 106-107 Remi Benali/Corbis, 107t NASA, 107cr China Daily/Reuters/Corbis, 108-109 Reuters/Corbis, 109t Galen Rowell/Corbis, 110-111 All NASA, 112–113 Rick Wilking/Reuters/Corbis, 114–115 Jim Reed/Corbis, 115tr Michael Ainsworth /Dallas Morning News/Corbis, 115bl Amy Ford/Dreamstime.com, 116-117 The Lawton/Corbis Sygma, 117tr Reuters/Corbis, 117br Corbis Sygma, 118–119 Corbis Sygma, 119tr Min. De Defense/Aut/Corbis Sygma, 120-121 Paul A. Souders/Corbis, 121cl NASA, 121tr Dreamstime.com, 122-123 Radu Sigheti/Reuters/Corbis, 123tr Radu Sigheti/Reuters/Corbis, 123cr Dreamstime.com/Nico Smit, 124-125 Mufty Munir/epa/Corbis, 124bl Jayanta Shaw/Reuters/Corbis, 125tl Jayanta Shaw/Reuters/Corbis, 126-127 Romeo Ranoco/Reuters/Corbis, 127tr Vic Kintanar/epa/Corbis, 127bl Francis Malasig/epa/Corbis, 128-129 Rick Friedman/Corbis, 129tr NASA, 129br Peter Morgan/Reuters/Corbis, 130-131 Wu Hong/epa/Corbis, 130bl iu Liqun/Corbis, 131cr Wu Hong/epa/Corbis, 132-133 Norman Godwin/Corbis, 133t Martin Gerten/epa/Corbis, 133br Reuters/Corbis, 134-135 Jim Reed/Corbis, 135tl Ron Sachs/CNP/Corbis, 135br Brendan Smialowski/epa/Corbis, 136-137 Josue Fernandez/epa/Corbis, 137tr NASA, 137bl Yann Arthus-Bertrand/Corbis, 138-139 Frithjof Hirdes/zefa/Corbis, 140-141 Bill Stormont/Corbis, 140bl Dreamstime.com/Freefly, 141tl Scott Liddell/Dreamstime.com, 141br Mika/zefa/Corbis, 142tr courtesy of Fairmount Weather Systems, 143t Maja Schon/Dreamstime.com, 143bl Michelle Bergkamp/Dreamstime.com, 144-145 Ashley Cooper/Corbis, 145tl Matej Krajcovic/Dreamstime.com, 145br courtesy of the Community Collaborative Rain, Hail and Snow Network, 146-147 Graham Neden; Ecoscene/Corbis, 146bl Dreamstime.com, 147t Dorothy Burrows; Eye Ubiquitous/Corbis, 147br Elnur Amikishiyev/Dreamstime.com, 148-149 NOAA/Corbis, 148b NASA, 149tr Armin Rose/Dreamstime.com, 149br John H. Clark/Corbis, 150-151 Fridmar Damm/zefa/Corbis, 150cr Jim Reed/Corbis, 151tr Dreamstime.com/Jerry Horn, 151bl Dreamstime.com/Brian Grant, 152-153 Corbis, 152bl NASA, 153t NASA, 153br NASA, 154-155 Visuals Unlimited, 154tr NASA, 154bl Dreamstime.com/Brett Williams, 155tr Rayna Canedy/Dreamstime.com, 156-157 Brian Snyder/Reuters/Corbis, 158-159 NASA, 160-161 Natalie Fobes/Corbis, 160bl Michael S. Yamashita/Corbis, 161tr Stephen Finn/Dreamstime.com, 161br Alejandro Ernesto/epa/Corbis, 162-163 Paul Edmondson/Corbis, 162bl Reuters/Corbis, 163tr David Hancock/Dreamstime.com, 163b Dreamstime.com, 164-165 Paul Almasy/Corbis, 166-167 Patrick Ward/Corbis, 166bl Dreamstime.com, 166bc Tt/Dreamstime.com, 166br Stefan Graeber/Dreamstime.com, 167br Richard Hamilton Smith/Corbis, 168-169 ML Sinibaldi/Corbis, 168bl Paulus Rusyanto/Dreamstime.com, 168br Robert Gill; Papilio/Corbis, 170-171 Ron Watts/Corbis, 170b Tall Tree Ltd, Shai Ginott/Corbis, 171bl Ron Sumners/Dreamstime.com, 172-173 Walter Geiersperger/Corbis, 172bl Dmitry Kozlov/Dreamstime.com, 173 Wolfgang Kaehler/Corbis, 174-175 Robert Francis/Robert Harding World Imagery/Corbis, 175tr David Brimm/Dreamstime.com, 175bl Peter Clark/Dreamstime.com, 176-177 Keren Su/Corbis, 177cl NASA, 178-179 Wolfgang Kaehler/Corbis, 178cr Dreamstime.com, 179br Jerry Horn/Dreamstime.com, 180-181 Anthony John West/Corbis, 180tr Dreamstime.com, 181bl Dreamstime.com/Eric Foltz, 182-183 Dreamstime.com/Andrew Barker, 182tr Dreamstie.com, 182b Peter Beck/Corbis, 184-185 Paul Almasy/Corbis, 184bl Andy Nowack/Dreamstime.com, 185tr David Chan/epa/Corbis, 185br NASA, 186-187 Jerzy Dabrowski/dpa/Corbis, 186tr Stefano Ginella/Dreamstime.com, 187br Dreamstime.com/Alessandro Bolis, 188-189 P. Wilson/zefa/Corbis, 189t pictures courtesy of Wavegen, 190-191 Paul Hanna/Reuters/Corbis, 192-193 Philippe Lissac/Godong/Corbis, 192bl Graça Victoria/Dreamstime.com, 193tl Gideon Mendel/Corbis, 193bl Darren Gilcher/Dreamstime.com, 194-195 Mark Wallheisser/Reuters/Corbis, 194tr Layne Kennedy/Corbis, 194bl Sean Sexton Collection/Corbis, 195tr Catherine Karnow/Corbis, 196-197 Emely/zefa/Corbis, 196tr Dreamstime.com, 197tr Ed Bock/Corbis, 198-199 Envision/Corbis, 198tr Dreamstime.com, 198bl Dreamstime.com/Dianne Maire, 200-201 Beat Glanzmann/zefa/Corbis, 201tr Dreamstime.com, 200bl Paul A. Souders/Corbis, 201tl Dreamstime.com/Marcus Brown, 202-203 Wu Hong/epa/Corbis, 203t Digital Vision, 203b Digital Vision, 204-205 Eva Miessler; Ecoscene/Corbis, 205tl Digital Vision, 205b Dreamstime.com, 206-207 NASA, 206t Patrick Ward/Corbis, 206b Digital Vision, 208-209 Stephen Coburn/Dreamstime.com, 209cl Roger Ressmeyer/Corbis, 210-211 NASA, 210bl Dreamstime.com, 211tl Andra Cerar/Dreamstime.com, 211bl Silvia Jansen/Dreamstime.com, 212-213 Douglas Peebles/Corbis, 212br Yves Herman/Reuters/Corbis, 213tr Dreamstime.com/Anthony Hathaway, 213bl Wolfgang Amri/Dreamstime.com, 214-215 Mark Emge/Dreamstime.com, 214bl Diego Cervo/Dreamstime.com, 215tr Petr Nad/Dreamstime.com, 215br Rainer/Dreamstime.com